CONTEXTS 1

The Beggar's Opera

CONTEXTS: SELECTED LITERARY WORKS IN THEIR HISTORICAL SETTINGS

General Editor

Maynard Mack

Contexts 1

THE BEGGAR'S OPERA

J. V. GUERINOT AND RODNEY D. JILG

ARCHON BOOKS
1976

1676267
DLC

11-13-84 JH

Library of Congress Cataloguing in Publication Data

Main entry under title:

The Beggar's opera.

    (Contexts—selected literary works in their historical
settings; 1)
      Bibliography: p.
      Includes index.
      1. Gay, John, 1685-1732. The beggar's opera. 2. Great
Britain—Intellectual life—18th century. 3. Great Britain
—Social conditions—18th century. I. Guerinot, Joseph
V. II. Jilg, Rodney D., 1939-
PR3473.B6B4   822'.5   75-29379
ISBN 0-208-01488-8

© 1976 by The Shoe String Press, Inc.
First published 1976 as an Archon Book,
an imprint of The Shoe String Press, Inc.,
Hamden, Connecticut 06514

Printed in the United States of America

CONTENTS

ACKNOWLEDGEMENTS

We wish to thank the Curators of the Bodleian Library and the Trustees of the British Museum for their kind permission to reproduce works in their possession. We owe a special debt to Miss Lesley Montgomery, Assistant Librarian, Worcester College, Oxford.

FOREWORD

Contexts is an experimental series intended for readers, teachers, and students who have discovered that literary works are known best when they are known in the setting of their own times as well as under the often radically changed conditions of ours. Each volume in the series seeks to illuminate a significant literary work by putting the reader in touch with primary historical materials contributing in an important way to the context of knowledge and feeling in which it was originally understood and enjoyed. The works selected for this attention are well known and widely disseminated in a variety of editions and reprints. It has therefore seemed unnecessary and unwise to take up space in reproducing these texts that could be more effectively used in enlarging the scope of the primary materials.

No method of supplying context for a literary work is entirely satisfactory. I believe, nevertheless, that the method chosen here has distinct advantages over the usual approach through editorial notes. For one thing, the impression left in the mind is far more powerful. To learn through editorial notes that the character of Peachum in Gay's *The Beggar's Opera* is drawn from an historical rogue named Jonathan Wild and refers to England's First Minister Robert Walpole; or that Swift's invention of the miniscule Lilliputians and gigantic Brobdingnagians in *Gulliver's Travels* owes something to the new dimensions opened to the imagination by the microscope and telescope; or that Pope's *The Rape of the Lock* begins with an invocation based on Homeric and Virgilian epic, is undoubtedly useful. But it is worlds away from discovering the underworld of Augustan London through contemporary documents in contemporary idiom, or reading for oneself about the houseflies that became alternatively great hairy monsters or tiny specks when viewed under microscope and telescope, or sampling the opening of the *Odyssey* or *Aeneid* at first hand.

Furthermore, access to a range of contemporary materials makes the reader's task as much more rewarding as it is challenging. No longer is his knowledge of—and therefore his ability to interpret—sources, antecedent traditions, current explanatory events, and the language of the age dependent on fragments of information provided in glosses and annotations. He confronts instead a wide horizon of possibility from which he may (and must) select what is useful to him, what will best explain the perplexing and clarify the apparently obscure. In this way, it becomes possible for him to participate actively in the recreation of the work and so to know a pleasure and exhilaration that reflect the author's own. What may also be stressed in this connection is that the degree and character of the work's originality, the nature of its unity as a whole with parts, the skill with which new things have been invented and old things transformed, can only be assessed by those in a position to examine at least a portion of the resources with which the author worked.

A final advantage that many teachers will respond to is the gathering of many rare and inaccessible documents in one convenient collection. Each collection, though inevitably limited by considerations of size and cost, makes feasible ways of teaching and kinds of questions-to-be-asked that are ordinarily only possible when one can send one's students to the stacks of a great library.

M. M.

INTRODUCTION

The *Beggar's Opera* is a deceptive work. Under its lucid surface lies a tangled undergrowth of allusion, parody, satire, and dry wit that must be penetrated if the *Opera* is to be either understood or enjoyed. It is, to begin with, a ballad opera, a genre that astonished in 1728 and now raises critical perplexities. Since it is the only ballad opera of genuine worth, we cannot learn much by comparing it to other English ballad operas. Yet it presumes our familiarity with the popular songs and lyrics of the day, and with the Italian operatic conventions that the Beggar assures us he is parodying. Its setting among the London criminal classes suggests further the usefulness of knowing something about the Augustan underworld, and the opening song, forcing us to compare thieves to statesmen, indicates clearly that political satire is also involved—but how much and what sort?

To gain the kind of perspective on which any informed reading of the *Opera* must rest, we obviously need to know as much as possible about the kinds of things Gay's own audiences knew, and that is the purpose of this book. We have reprinted here, in four chapters, as many contemporary documents relating to the literary, criminal, political, and musical backgrounds of the work as space would allow, combining them with a commentary that seeks to show the relevance of each to our apprehension of Gay's purpose. These four chapters are followed by two having to do with the *Opera's* reception and the storm of criticism that it raised both for its supposed immorality and its actual revolutionary challenge to Establishment mentality in all times and places.

For students, we believe this approach to the problem of interpretation and criticism has the unique advantage of supplying necessary information in an entertaining as well as illuminating way, while stimulating their own imaginations to make the linkages that a contemporary spectator would have made. For teachers, it has the further advantage it seems to us, of allowing classtime to be spent not on historical explication but on substantive issues having to do with Gay's period and ours, with human nature and the organization of society, and with the author's extraordinary talent for assimilating the most ephemeral persons and situations into enduring art.

1. The Literary Background

Johnson stressed Gay's originality in writing *The Beggar's Opera* when he said in his *Life of Gay*, "Much . . . must be allowed to the author of a new species of composition . . . . We owe to Gay the Ballad Opera." All that Gay had done, however, was what every great artist does: he had created something new by using what was lying at hand.

Ballad opera, the genre to which Gay gave its only distinguished specimen, is simply a comedy with songs set to familiar tunes. Insofar as *The Beggar's Opera* is an "opera," it has a few obvious parallels with Purcell's operas, the most famous of their kind, which were also spoken dramas with songs and symphonic music. Purcell's operas, however, were heroical and romantic five-act affairs (*King Arthur, The Fairy Queen*), and their music was not at all derived from traditional airs. The gorgeous baroque world of Purcell, loftily inhabited by great figures human as well as divine, has little to do with the realism of Gay, unless one were to argue, perhaps not altogether perversely, that its preoccupation with heroic posturing is reflected in Gay's mock-heroic portrayal of Macheath.

But the stage's heroicomical treatment of grandiose attitudes and aspirations goes at least as far back as Beaumont's *The Knight of the Burning Pestle*, first performed ca. 1608. Perhaps the most famous of all heroicomical burlesques came later in the same century—Buckingham's *The Rehearsal*, aimed at the heroic tragedy of the Restoration, especially Dryden's, and anticipating Gay in its use of a number of broadside ballads. A form yet closer to *The Beggar's Opera* is that of the French *comédies en vaudeville*. These were performed, in opposition to the established Comédie Française, at the Théâtres de la Foire, especially the Foire St.

Laurent and the Foire St. Germain. and acted almost entirely by Italians who had inherited the tradition of the *commedia dell' arte*. As the form of the *comédies en vaudeville* developed, dialogue in prose became generously interspersed with lyrics set to well-known tunes—exactly the form of ballad opera, which these comedies also resemble in the fun they make of highly stylized acting techniques and the manners of opera singers. Many, however, use elaborate stage machines, exotic settings, and fantastic and marvellous plots, and thus differ sharply in tone and content from English ballad opera. Gay could easily have seen samples of this genre on one of his visits to Paris in 1717 and 1719, or in London, where there were numerous performances between 1718 and 1725.

Just as there exist literary antecedents for the form of the *Opera*, so there are earlier parallels for its content. With his rogue characters, Gay falls into the tradition of English low life literature that begins as early as Chaucer's Miller and Summoner. We might think especially of the two parts of *Henry IV*, where Falstaff and his gang, drinking and wenching at the Boar's Head, robbing travelers at Gadshill, living disreputably and endearingly off their society, are in some respects Elizabethan counterparts of the Augustan Peacham and Company—both gangs serving to satirize the corruption of their societies. Falstaff's thievery on the road is, Shakespeare's play insists, the counterpart to Henry's theft of the throne from Richard II and the would-be theft of it from Henry by Hotspur and his allies; Peachum's attachment to money, Gay equally insists, is matched in Walpole's materialism. In each case, England is sick because its leadership is sick, and that sickness, spreading from high places, is reflected in the behavior of the rogues and threatens the whole fabric of society.

There is a further interesting parallel to the *Opera* in Richard Brome's *A Jovial Crew*, first acted in 1641. This offers us a low-life setting, beggar-characters, a highly romanticized beggar-kingdom, along with some charming songs. Still closer home is the rogue literature of Gay's own

4

time and the concurrent interest in famous criminals, espe-
ically Jonathan Wild and Jack Sheppard. Criminal biogra-
phies, a genre that goes back to the 16th century, were at the
height of their popularity. These lives of convicted felons
who were to be hanged at Tyburn are with few exceptions
highly stereotyped and depressingly sordid accounts of
villainy, vice, disease, and eleventh hour repentance. They
were sold to the crowd before the execution for a penny or
two, supposedly to increase the moral value of the occasion.
Three such were issued in connection with the execution of
Joseph Blake, six for Jack Sheppard, eight for Jonathan Wild.
Captain Alexander Smith's *A Compleat History of the Lives
and Robberies of the Most Notorious Highwaymen*, which
was first published in 1714 and by 1719 had gone through
five editions, treated 137 criminals in this moralizing way.
Some of the interest spilled over into the theatre. We reprint
excerpts from the plays preceding *The Beggar's Opera*
which treat of Newgate and criminals.

Le Tableau du Mariage, a *comédie en vaudeville*, was performed in London during May, 1726. The scene is Paris, and the family, the Pepins, are bourgeois. The play focuses on the question of whether Diamantine, the niece of the Pepins, is to marry Octave or not. At the end of fifteen scenes and twenty-seven songs (set to identifiable tunes) she decides not to; the piece is then finished by the *Troupe de Masques & d'amis invitez aux noces.*

Le Tableau du Mariage has some remarkable similarities to Gay's *Opera*: they both have many rapidly changing scenes; they both use songs set to existing airs; the dialogue in both is short, witty, and frequently satiric; and both end with a dance. *Le Tableau du Mariage* is, in effect, a ballad opera some years earlier than Gay's.

Le Tableau du Mariage, Scene I complete, the first of fifteen scenes, from what is (apparently) the first printing, Tome II, 1721: [278]-283 in Lesage, [A.R.] and D'Orneval, Le Theatre De La Foire, Ou L'Opera Comique. 10 vols. Paris, 1721-1737.

ACTEURS.

M. PEPIN, Bourgeois de Paris.

Mde. PEPIN, sa Femme.

DIAMANTINE, leur Niéce.

OCTAVE, Amant de Diamantine.

OLIVETTE, Suivante de Diamantine.

ARLEQUIN, Valet d'Octave.

SCARAMOUCHE, Confiseur.

M. MINUTIN, Notaire.

M. FRANCOEUR, Marchand de rubans.

TROUPE de Masques & d'Amis invitez aux nôces.

SYMPHONISTES.

La Scene est à Paris.

LE TABLEAU
DU
MARIAGE.

 E Theâtre represente une façade de Maison dans le fond, & un Jardin orné de statuës dans les aîles.

SCENE PREMIERE.

DIAMANTINE, OLIVETTE.

OLIVETTE.

AIR 171. (*D'Atis.*)

Sangaride, ce jour est un grand jour pour vous.

Vous allez donc enfin signer les articles de votre mariage. Là, vous sentez-vous la main assez ferme...?

DIAMANTINE.

Je ne sais.

OLIVETTE.

Je ne fais! Ouais! Ce je ne fais préfage une rechute d'incertitude.

AIR 40. (*Si dans le mal qui me poffede*)

En verité, je vous admire.
Comment! Après que devant moy
Octave a reçu votre foy,
Vous voilà prête à vous dédire!
Vous trahiriez votre ferment!
Fi! Vous avez le cœur Normand!

DIAMANTINE.

Ma chere Olivette, apren ce qui m'effraye.

OLIVETTE.

Voyons.

DIAMANTINE.

J'ai fait un fonge épouvantable. J'ai vû deux Pigeons qui fortoient d'un colombier...

OLIVETTE.

Deux Pigeons qui fortoient d'un colombier! Voilà un commencement de rêve qui fait trembler.

DIAMANTINE.

Ils fe font arrêtez dans un champ. La

femelle careffoit le mâle, qui bien loin de répondre à fes careffes, lui a donné deux coups de bec en fureur, & s'eft envolé.

OLIVETTE.

Ah! le vilain mâle!

DIAMANTINE.

Ce fpectacle m'a réveillée. J'ai regardé mon fonge comme un avis que le Ciel me donne de me défier des hommes. Je ne fignerai point le contract. Je veux auparavant effayer encore le cœur d'Octave, & lui demander un délay.

OLIVETTE.

AIR I. (*Réveillez-vous, belle Endormie*)

Vous aimez, & l'on vous adore;
Pourquoi ces bizarres effais?
Je n'ai point vû de fille encore
Demander de pareils délais.

DIAMANTINE.

Tu me connois. Tu fais que j'ai pour le mariage une répugnance naturelle.

OLIVETTE.

Oh! Dites furnaturelle, s'il vous plaît.

A I R 99. (*D'une main je tiens mon pot*)

Le principe eſt contre vous,
    Avouez-le entre nous.
On peut bien trouver dans des Belles
Des répugnances naturelles
Pour certains Maris, *concedo*;
    Mais pour l'hymen, *nego*.

D I A M A N T I N E.

Tes plaiſanteries ſont hors de ſaiſon.
J'aime Octave; mais je ne veux pas être
malheureuſe.

O L I V E T T E.

A I R 73. (*Dedans nos Bois il y a un Hermite*)

Que fera-t-on du feſtin qu'on apprête?
    Que diront vos Amis?
Ils vont bientôt s'aſſembler pour la fête;
    Le bal leur eſt promis:
On rira bien de cette contredanſe.
    Je perds patience,
        Moy,
    Je perds patience.

D I A M A N T I N E.

Je devine ce qui vous fait perdre pa-
tience: Vous craignez que le retardement

de mes noces ne recule les vôtres; Mais
r'aſſurez-vous, Mademoiſelle Olivette;
vous pouvez dès aujourd'hui épouſer Arlequin.

A I R 105. (*La bonne avanture, ô gay*)

Là-deſſus ſois ſans effroy.
    Deplus, je te jure
Que les apprêts faits pour moy,
Mon enfant, ſeront pour toy.

O L I V E T T E, *ſautant de joye.*

La bonne avanture,
    O gay,
La bonne avanture!

D I A M A N T I N E.

Ah! voilà Monſieur Minutin mon fleg-
matique Notaire.

O L I V E T T E.

Et voici le bruſque Monſieur Francœur
votre Marchand de rubans. Ce ſont deux
caractères bien oppoſez.

Christopher Bullock's *Woman's Revenge: Or, A Match in Newgate* (1715) has a cast of professional rogues, and its setting is either directly outside Newgate or in the prison. Vizard, the chief villain of the piece, pronounces that the world is out of joint because of "the Corruption of the Age" (I.i). Though Bullock's cynicism falls far short of Gay's satire, there are similarities in the way they use low-born rogues to attack and question high-born rogues. Bullock, like Gay after him, chooses Newgate as his primary symbol for the "corruption of the age."

Woman's Revenge: Or, A Match in Newgate . . . The Second Edition . . . London: Printed for J. Roberts in Warwick-Lane. 1728. Pp. [1]-8. The first third of Act I of this three act play, first acted in 1715 and revived in 1727.

A
Match in NEWGATE.
A
COMEDY.

ACT I. SCENE I.

Enter Freeman, *and* Mixum *the Vintner.*   1

Freeman. HOW now, *Robin Mixum!* What makes thee in this Confusion? What's the Matter?

Mixum. O, Sir, the moſt villainous Piece of Roguery,— not of my own, Sir,— but that Rogue of all Rogues, *Vizard*'s committing: 2 I'll tell you, Sir, how it was; that Villain, *Vizard*, who has more Tricks than ·a Jeſuit, and wou'd make an Aſs of the Devil, came to my Houſe one Night, and with him a Woman, whom he told me he had married, and that ſhe was a great Fortune; upon which I grew extremely civil: He order'd the Cloth 3 to be laid; which was done while you cou'd Whiſtle, beſpoke a Supper, which was upon

B   the

---

1. Stage Direction. *Vintner*: an innkeeper selling wine
2. *Vizard*'s: vizard: a mask to conceal or disguise the face
3. Cloth: table cloth

the Table in a Trice: He gave me a Bill of twenty Pounds, and defired the Money of me; the Goldfmith living too far to fend to at that Time, I willingly gave him the Money,
4 took his Bill, and withdrew: Then enters a
5 blind Harper, and cries, Do you lack any Mufick? He cries, play; the Harper uncafes,
6 the Drawer is nodded out, who obeys, believing he wou'd be private with the Gentlewoman; and 'tis *Sam's* Part, you know, Sir, to wink at fuch Things.

Free. Right, and civil.

Mix. Well, Sir, having eat the Supper, and perceiving none in the Room but the blind Harper, whofe Eyes Heaven had fhut from beholding Wickednefs, opens the Cafement to the Street, very patiently packs up
7 my Plate, naturally thrufts the Woman out of the Window, and himfelf, with the moft acute Dexterity, leaps after her: The blind
8 Harper plays on, bids the empty Difhes, much good may do them, and plays on ftill; the Drawer returns, cries, D'ye call, Sir? But out, alas, the Birds were flown, Sir, flown; Laments were rais'd.——

Free. Which did not pierce the Heavens.

Mix. Sam cries out; my Wife, in the Bar, hears the Noife; fhe bawls out, I heard her, and thunder'd, the Boys flew like Lightning, and all was in Confufion; my Plate being gone, and the Thief after it, I bethought me of my Bill, ran with all fpeed to the Goldfmiths to receive my Money;——— but alas, the Bill prov'd forg'd, I was feiz'd, *Vizard* run away, my Word wou'd not be taken, I was found guilty of Forgery, loft my Reputation,

---

4. his Bill: on the goldsmith
5. Harper: a harp player
6. Drawer: a tapster in a tavern
7. Plate: table-ware
8. bids: asks or begs [here, for money]

tation, and was put in the Pillory for being cheated.

Free. Was it impossible to find him?

Mix. Sir, he walks invisible; you might as soon find Truth in a Gamester, Sincerity in a Lawyer, or Honour in a Poet; he changes his Dress and his Lodgings, as often as a Whore does her Name and her Lovers: I'll e'en go home, and comfort myself and my Wife; and for that Rogue *Vizard.* I hope I shall live to see him hang'd in Hemp of his own beating.　　　　　　　　　　　　[*Exit.*　9

Free. This is a most exemplary piece of Justice: This Vintner I know to be a Knave, one that has Cunning enough to cheat all that put Faith in him, and Wit enough to avoid the Punishment of his own Crimes, but by the Malignity of Fortune, is ever suffering for other Men's Roguery: Ha, here comes the ambo-dexterous Knave! So, Mr. *Vizard,* you are in great Haste, upon a hot Scent, I find, in Quest of your Prey; What Darling of Fortune are you going to run down?

Viz. Fie, Mr. *Freeman,* you shou'd not judge so hard of a poor Man.

Free. The Accusation of *Robin Mixum* the Vintner, concerning the forg'd Bill, will give your Acquaintance just Cause to distrust your Morals.

Viz. Sir, there is not a greater Rogue in the whole Company of Vintners.

Free. The World, I believe, is pretty well apprised of his Honesty; but his being a Knave, is no Proof of your Innocence; you

　　　　　　　　B 2　　　　　　　　　shou'd

---

9. own beating: preparing hemp for rope was a common task of prisoners

shou'd have appear'd in Court, and disprov'd
his scandalous Accusation.

Viz. Villainy, Sir, is ever most fertile in
Invention, while Innocence often suffers, and
by Surprize is made uncapable of Defence:
The Rogue knew very well I did not dare to
confront him in Court, by reason I had a
swinging Action out against me; so he took
the Advantage of my Misfortune, to vindi-
cate his Reputation, by the Aspersion of
mine: The Villain deprives me of my Livelihood, by unjustly possessing an Estate of
two hundred Pounds *per Annum*, that my Father mortgag'd to him for a thousand Pounds,
which he spent again in his House, and had
nothing for it but bad Wine and gross Flattery, and now he wou'd rob me of my good
Character.

Free. Which you have been a Stranger to
these twelve Months.—— Come, come, your
scandalous Practices, your Cheats and Tricks
are pretty well known; consider, you have
but few Friends, little Reputation, and less
Money; and if you shou'd be taken hold on
by the Law, and convicted, you'd hardly e-
scape its Punishment.

Viz. That's owing to the Corruption of the
Age: For as you seem to intimate, few Men,
indeed, suffer for Dishonesty, but for Poverty,
many: The greatest Part of Mankind being
Rogues within, or without the Law, so that
little Thieves are hang'd for the Security of
great ones. Take my Word, Sir, there are
greater Rogues ride in their own Coaches,
than any that walk on Foot; a poor Fellow
shall

---

10. swinging: hanging

fhall be hang'd for Stealing to fupport Life, while many folemn Villains, with furpercillious Faces, and brufh'd Beavers, that plunder whole Families, are complimented with the Title of Right Worfhipful.   11

Free. I wonder that a Man of your Underftanding, and one that has run thro' fo good a Fortune, can be contented with a Livelihood, got by fuch fcandalous Practices; 'tis a Difgrace both to your Birth and Education: Have you no Friend that——

Viz. When I had Money, I had many Profeffors; but Neceffity is the Touchftone of Friends. I have learn'd, Sir, at a fevere Expence, that Friendfhip is but a Shadow that attends the Sunfhine of our Profperity, which once overclouded, with adverfe Fortune, the other ftrait becomes invifible.   12

    13

Free. I am too well affur'd of your Misfortune in that Refpect, but endeavour to maintain a good Reputation, and you ftand fair for Preferment; you are very well qualify'd for a Place, and have Merit enough to countenance your Pretentions.

Viz. Sir, with fubmiffion, I find you have ftudied Books more than Men, you know what fhou'd give a Man a Pretention to prefer himfelf, but are ignorant in what does; alas, Sir, the antient Theory of Vertue is quite revers'd, and he that has the moft Money is now the worthieft Man: Every Thing is to be fold; both ends of the Town are become Markets, and Confciences rife and fall, at *Weftminfter*, as Stocks do in *'Change-Alley.*   14,15

Free. You are very Satirical, but I have made an Obfervation, that the greateft Knaves

B 3   are

---

11. Beavers: hats of beaver's fur, more commonly, in the 18th century, made of rabbit's fur.
12. Professors: those who profess [friendship]
13. strait: immediately
14. *Westminster*: Parliament, in the west of London
15. *'Change Alley*: Early equivalent of New York's 'Wall Street,' in the east of London

are the moſt ſevere Judges; they view all
Mankind in the falſe mirror of their own
Actions; and when they can't defend theit
Villanies, think to extenuate them by plead-
ing the Example of their Betters.

Viz. You miſtake me, Sir, I am of a contrary Opinion, for if Example cou'd juſtify
Actions, there cou'd be no Thieves; Poſſeſ-
ſion wou'd then be the only Right; Children
might turn their Fathers out of Doors, Subjects call their Soveraigns to Account, Uſur-
pers plead a Divine-Right, and the greateſt
Villanies wou'd become lawful; I cou'd ſay
more, Sir, but great Men's Vices muſt be ſa-
16   cred—— where *Scandalum Magnatum* is puniſh'd with ſuch Severity, and Money is an Argument to prove Black White, poor Men dare
not ſpeak the Truth of their Betters: In this
Age there are more Funeral Sermons, than
Satires.

Free. I can't ſay but in ſome Meaſure your
Obſervation is juſt, few Men having the Senſe
to bear honeſt Satire as they ought.

Viz. Sir, give me leave to recommend this
ſmall Treatiſe to your peruſal, 'tis call'd,
Beware of a Knave; 'tis a true Deſcription of
Mankind, written originally in *Spaniſh*, by
an excellent Maſter, in the thriving art of
17   *Chicane.*   *(Gives him a Book.*

Free. What ſhou'd I do with it? Think'ſt
thou I am ſo baſe to ſtudy ſuch vile Arts, or
ſo indigent as to practiſe 'em?

Viz. I mean no Reflection on your Honour
18   or Fortune; but in theſe couzening Times,
'tis more neceſſary to ſtudy other Men, than
our ſelves; and 'tis proper to know falſe Dice,
tho'

---

16. *Scandalum Magnatum*: defamatory speech or writing against a peer or high
official
17. *Chicane*: trickery
18. couzening: cheating by trickery, defrauding

tho' a Man ſcorns to make uſe of them: Ay,
Sir, there's many a Man, perhaps that you
think honeſter than myſelf, wou'd, if Opportunity ſerv'd, look in your Face, and pick
your Pocket.—— Time and Experience will
confirm you in the Truth of what I ſay:
[*Picks his Pocket.*] The Age is quite alter'd,
Intereſt is now the Standard of moſt Men's
Actions, and every Thing accounted Vertuous
that promotes it ; a Man's Proſperity is now
the only Mark of his Wiſdom and Honeſty,
while ill Fortune and old Cloaths, make a
Man ſuſpected for a Fool, or a Rogue: Beſides, Sir, for a Man to aim at Preferment,
with nothing but a good Reputation, wou'd
be as fruitleſs as to ſue for an Eſtate in *Forma*
Pauperis: Merit, Sir, gives a Man no Title
to Advancement ; Preferment, Sir, like a
Common-Whore, was ever courted with Pre-
ſents.

Free. I wiſh it were otherwiſe,—— however, the worſt of Times can't make an Im-
preſſion on true Vertue, for that's a Rock,
which ſtands immoveable in the moſt violent
Storms of Fortune :—— There's ſomewhat
for you, and all I have about me Faith at preſent : Be honeſt, and I ſhall be proud to ſerve
you.   [*Exit.*
Viz. A civil Fellow Faith ; I pick his Pocket, and he generouſly rewards my Ingenuity:—— Be honeſt, ha, ha, ha, I thank you,
Sir, I love no ſuch ſtarving Vertue: I ſhou'd
be proud to ſerve you! No, I deſpiſe a Life
dependant on others Courteſy: There are
Fools enow in the World for witty Men to
ſtrike their Fortunes out of, and he only de-
                    B 4   ſerves

19

---

19. *Forma Pauperis:* 'one allowed, on account of poverty, to ſue or defend in a court
   of law without paying costs' *O.E.D.*

ſerves to live, that has an Art, to extract Gold
out of Lead.   [*Exit.*

As the crime wave in London in the 1720's continued to swell, several plays were written to capitalize on the notoriety of Jack Sheppard, the thief and prison-breaker extraordinary.[1] The first of these, a pantomime, *Harlequin Sheppard*, was printed and produced in 1724. Written by John Thurmond, and produced at the Theatre Royal, Drury Lane, it was booed off the stage the first night. The pantomime (which is very elementary) deserves attention because Gay's "Newgate's Garland: Being A New Ballad" was used in it, to be sung to the tune of "Packington's Pound." Joseph Blake, otherwise Blueskin, a companion of Sheppard's who had been betrayed by Wild, had attacked Wild in the courtroom and wounded him in the throat with a penknife. The ballad shows Gay's early awareness of Sheppard's world, a world that interested him strongly enough to provoke him to the writing of new lyrics to an old song. He would several years later use the same technique for his songs for *The Beggar's Opera.*

---

1. For Sheppard and Wild see Chapter II.

Harlequin Sheppard. A Night Scene In Grotesque Characters . . . By John Thurmond . . . London, Printed: And Sold by J. Roberts in Warwick-Lane, and A. Dodd at the Peacock without Temple-Bar. 1724. The complete pantomine, omitting the introduction (a life of Sheppard).

Harlequin Sheppard.

THE Curtain draws up, and difcovers *Sheppard* in the Room
call'd the *Caftle* of *Newgate*, 1
with his Fetters on, and padlock'd to
the Ground. The Mufic plays a Plain-
tive Tune. He feems ruminating on his
hard Condition; and viewing with great
Concern the Place of his Abode, finds
a fmall Nail, with which he unlocks
the Padlock that holds his Chains fix'd
to the Floor. Seems pleas'd; attempts
to get up the Chimney, but is fuppos'd
to be hinder'd by an Iron Bar that goes
acrofs the Infide. While he is doing
this, one of the *Keepers* enters and difcovers him without his Irons, at which
he

1. *Newgate*: the great London prison

he feems much furpris'd, runs out, and
calls the reft, who immediately enter,
place *Sheppard* on his Stool again, ma-
nacle him, and load him with much
heavier Chains than the former, and
fix him again to the Staple. They go
out, and one returns with a Pie, which
he gives him, and leaves him. The Mufic changes. When *Sheppard*'s alone,
he opens the Pie, and takes out his Implements, and goes to Work. Firft
he undoes his Manacles with his Teeth,
and then twifts one of his Chains afunder; after that ties up his Fetters to
2 his Wafte with his Garters, goes to
work on the Chimney, and in a little
time picks out the Bricks with the broken Piece of his Chain, and afcends
the Breach.

The SCENE changes to a Room
call'd the *Red-Room* in *Newgate*, where
he is again difcover'd coming in thro'
the Breach. He feems to rejoice, and
goes to the Door of the *Red-Room*, and

with

2. Waste: waist

with his Implements forces the Lock,
and goes out.

The SCENE changes to *the Street.*
Several Prifoners pafs over the Stage
with the Keepers of *Newgate.* Among
the Prifoners, are fuppos'd to be *Blue-* 3
skin, *Julian* the *Black,* &c. Several 4
People follow 'em as it were to the
Old Baily to receive their Tryal. The
Mufic changes. Enter two People as
from the *Old Baily* in Surprize, one 5
with a Pen-knife in his Hand, who
makes Signs that one of the Prifoners
had cut a Man's Throat. Immediately
the Prifoners Re-enter, and *Blueskin*
exulting, imagining that he had cut
Jonathan Wild's Throat effectually.
Some of the Keepers bring acrofs *Jonathan Wild,* with his Throat cut. Some
of the Prifoners fing the following Song.

SONG:

---

3. *Blueskin*: see headnote
4. *Julian the Black*: unidentified—possibly a made-up name
5. *Old Baily*: the criminal court

S O N G:

Sung by Mr. HARPER.

To the Tune of *Packington's Pound.*

I.

*Y*E *Fellows of Newgate whose Fingers are nice,*
6   *In diving in Pockets, or cogging of Dice,*
Ye Sharpers so rich, who can buy off the Noose,
Ye honest poor Rogues, who die in your Shoes,
     Attend, and draw near,
     Good News ye shall hear,
  How Jonathan's *Throat was cut from Ear to Ear;*
How Blueskin's *sharp Penknife hath set you at Ease,*
And every Man round me, may Rob, if they please.

II.

When to the Old Baily *this* Blueskin *was led,*
He held up his Hand, his Indictment was read:
Loud rattled his Chains. Near him Jonathan *stood,*
For full forty Pounds was the Price of his Blood.
     Then hopeless of Life,
     He drew his Penknife,
  And made a sad Widow of Jonathan's *Wife;*
But forty Pounds paid her, her Grief shall appease,
And every Man round me, may Rob, if they please.

III. *Knaves*

---

6. cogging of Dice: cheating at dice

III.

[tions,

Knaves of Old to hide Guilt, by their cunning Inven-
Call'd Briberies Grants, and plain Robberies Penfions:
Phyficians and Lawyers (who took their Degrees,
To be learned Rogues) call'd their Pilfering, Fees: 7
   Since this happy Day,
   Now every Man may,
  Rob (as fafe as in Office) upon the High-way,
For Blueskin's *fharp Penknife hath fet you at Eafe,*
And every Man round me, may Rob, if they pleafe.

IV.

Some cheat in the Cuftoms, fome rob the Excife,
But he who robs both is efteemed moft Wife;
Church-Wardens, who always have dreaded the Halter,
As yet, only venture to fteal from the Altar:
   But now to get Gold
   They may be more Bold,
  And rob on the High-way, fince Jonathan's *Cold;*
For Blueskin's *fharp Penknife hath fet you at Eafe,*
And every Man round me, may Rob, if they pleafe.

V.

[Hands,

Some, by Publick Revenues, which pafs'd thro' their
Have purchas'd clean Houfes, and bought dirty Lands:
Some to fteal from a Charity think it no Sin, 8
Which, at home (fays the Proverb) does always begin;
   But if ever you be
   Affign'd a Truftee,
  Treat not Orphans like Mafters of the Ch——ry, 9
But take the High-way, and more honeftly fzize,
For every Man round me, may Rob, if they pleafe.
    C   VI. *What*

---

7. *Pilfering*: petty theft
8. *to steal from a charity*: alluding to the embezzlement of funds set aside for the relief of the poor.
9. Ch_ry: Chancery: 'the court of the Lord Chancellor of England, the highest court of judicature next to the House of Lords.' *O.E.D.* Orphans were made wards of Chancery and frequently cheated out of their estates by its lawyers.

VI.

What a Pother has here been, with Wood *and his Braſs,*
Who wou'd modeſtly make a few Halfpennies paſs?
The Patent is good, and the Precedent's old,
For Diomede *changed his Copper for Gold.*
       But if Ireland *deſpiſe*
       The new Halfpennies,
   With more Safety to rob on the Road, I adviſe.
For Blueskin's *ſharp Penknife has ſet you at Eaſe,*
And every Man round me, may Rob, if they pleaſe.

After the Song is ended they go out, and the SCENE changes to the Outſide of *Newgate. Sheppard* is diſcover'd coming from the Top of *Newgate* upon the *Turner's* Leads by the help of a Blanket.

The SCENE changes, to the Outſide of the *Turner's* Houſe. The Stage is entirely darken'd. The *Turner's* Maid is diſcover'd walking backward and forward in the Room, as if about Buſineſs, with a Candle in her Hand. *Sheppard* is ſeen cautiouſly walking behind her. She hears the Clink of his Irons, and diſcovers the utmoſt Surprize, looks about, at which *Sheppard* retires; ſhe ſeeing nothing, goes off frighted. *Sheppard*

10. *Pother*: trouble, fuss
11. Wood *and his Brass*: William Wood was granted in 1722 a royal patent to coin, for use in Ireland, a large quantity of copper money; Swift protested the scheme in *The Drapier's Letters.*
12. Diomede: In Bk IV of *The Iliad* Diomedes exchanges his brass arms for Glaucus's golden ones.
13. *Turner's* Leads: the lead roof of the adjoining house belonging to a Mr. Turner.

26

pard follows her. The Maid is difcover'd in another Room, fhe undreffes
herfelf, puts out the Candle, and is
fuppos'd to go to Bed. The Windows
of this laft Scene are tranfparent, fo
that the Perfons in the Action are feen
by the Spectators thro' the Window.

The SCENE changes to the Out-
fide of *Newgate*. *Sheppard* comes out
at the Door of the *Turner*'s Houfe,
and goes into a Coach waiting for him
under the Gate, which immediately
drives away. The Keepers enter in a
great Surprize and Confternation, as
having juft found out *Sheppard*'s Efcape. They point up to the Top of
Newgate, to the Blanket which *Sheppard* had left behind him, and knock
at the *Turner*'s Door. The Maid comes
out, and feems furpriz'd. She goes in
again, and the Keepers retire.

The SCENE changes to *Drury-* 14
Lane. The Sign of the 3 Bowls hung
out. *Sheppard* enters merrily, goes to
the Pawn-broker's, and is fuppos'd to

C 2   break

---

14. *Drury-Lane:* famous for its proftitutes

break it open. Enters again with a Bundle, and goes out, rejoicing.

The SCENE changes to *Newtoner's-Lane*. *Sheppard* enters, and breaks open the Cellar of a Houfe, and goes in. The Mob follow him immediately, and run down after him into the Cellar. He breaks out into 1 the Street thro' the Iron Grate of the Cellar; fome follow him the fame way, and the reft come up again. *Sheppard* finding himfelf hard purfu'd, tears down the Shutter of a Window, and throws himfelf thro' the Glafs into the Houfe. The Mob purfue him, and enter the Houfe thro' the Window. *Sheppard* comes out from another part of the Houfe, and the Mob following him hard, he throws himfelf into a Window up one pair of Stairs of the adjacent Houfe, and from thence breaks thro' the Cieling, gets on the Top of the Houfe, and throws down the Tyles upon the People below. They to avoid 'em run down into the Cellar; he immedi-

---

15. *Newtoner's-Lane*: another name for Lewkner's Lane (mentioned in *The Beggar's Opera*, II.iii), where Jonathan Wild had run a brothel

immediately comes down, and bars
'em in. One of 'em is endeavouring
to come out of the Cellar-grate, whom
he knocks down, and goes off.

The S C E N E changes to *Clare-* 16
Market, and difcovers a Butcher's Shop.
Sheppard comes in very merry, and
goes to purchafe fome of the Meat.
While he is employ'd with the Butcher, an Ale-houfe Boy comes in, with
Potts over his Shoulder, and difcovering *Sheppard*, retires. *Sheppard* and
the Butcher go off together.

The S C E N E changes to a Room
in an Ale-houfe. *Frisky Moll* enters, 17
and feems to be pleas'd, as having heard
of *Sheppard*'s Efcape. *Sheppard* comes
in, and difcovering himfelf to her, fhe's
mightily rejoic'd. They drink together,
and after fome time dance. While
they are in high Mirth, the Ale-houfe
Boy appears with the Conftable and o-
thers, and feize *Sheppard*. *Frisky
Moll* makes Refiftance, but they carry
him off: And the Entertainment con-
cludes with   A

16. *Clare-Market*: a market between Lincoln's Inn Fields and the Strand, noted for
    its butchers
17. *Frisky Moll*: unidentified; she sings the canting song that follows. Sheppard
    after his escape was sheltered by Kate Cook, alias Mackaine.

A CANTING SONG,

Sung by FRISKY MOLL.

The Words by Mr. *Harper.*

FRom *Priggs that snaffle the Prancers strong,* (1)
　To you of the Peter L*a*y, (2)
I Pray now listen a while to my Song,
　How my Boman *he hick'd away.* (3)

He broke thro' all Ruhhs in the Whitt, (4)
　And chiv'd his Darbies in twain; (5)
But fileing of a Rumbo Ken, (6)
　My Boman *is snabbled again.* (7)

I Frisky Moll, *with my Rum Coll,* (8)
　Wou'd Grub in a Bowzing Ken; (9)
But ere for the Scran he had tipt the Cole, (10)
　The Harman *he came in.* (11)

(1) Gentlemen of the Pad. (2) Those that break
Shop-Glasses, or cut Portmanteaus behind Coaches.
(3) Her Rogue had got away. (4) *Newgate,* or
any other Prison. (5) Saw'd his Chains in two.
(6) Robbing a Pawn-broaker's Shop. (7) Taken
again. (8) Clever Thief. (9) Wou'd eat in an
Ale-house. (10) Before the Reckoning was paid.
(11) The Constable.

A

A Famble (12), *a Tattle* (13), *and two Popps,* (14)
   Had my Boman *when he was ta'en;*
But had he not Bowz'd in the Diddle Shops, (15)
   He'd still been in Drury-Lane.

(12) A Ring. (13) A Watch. (14) A Pair of
Pistols. (15) Geneva Shops.

F I N I S.

Among possible dramatic influences on Gay must be reckoned *The Prison-Breaker; Or, The Adventures Of John Sheppard*, printed in 1725, but never acted. This farce by an unknown author is built around Sheppard and Jonathan Wile, a thief-taker, obviously meant for Jonathan Wild. The rest of the cast suggests characters in *The Beggar's Opera*: Nym (see *Henry V*) and File are close to Gay's Nimming Ned and Filch; Sheppard's escape and apprehension resemble Macheath's escape and recapture. The thieves in *The Prison-Breaker* style themselves "Rogues of Honour," much as do Macheath's gang (ii.i). Whether Gay knew *The Prison-Breaker* or not remains unclear; what is sure is that his *Opera* is vastly superior. The anonymous play's Sheppard is little more than a drunken thug, its moralizing the stalest possible. The following brief extract should suffice to give its flavour:

The Prison-Breaker; Or, The Adventures of John Sheppard. A Farce . . . London: Printed for A. Moore, near St. Pauls. 1725. [1p], pp. 1-5, about the first fifth of the first act of this two act play.

Dramatis Personæ.

Sheppard,
File,
Nym, } Thieves.
Hempseed,
Bulk,

Rust, } Two Gaolers.
Careful,

Jonathan Wile, a Thief-taker.
Coax-thief, Master of a Publick House, where the Thieves resort.
A Gentleman.
Blunder, an *Irishman.*
Dr. *Anatomy.*
A Quaker.
A Welsh *Lawyer.*

Mrs. *Poorlean.*
Mrs. *Coax-thief.*

Constable, Watch, &c.

(1)

ACT I.

SCENE *NEWGATE.*

Enter Rust, *and* Careful.

Mrs. Poorlean *sitting at a Distance, with Bottles, Glasses, and Quart Potts on Table before her.*

CAREFUL.

Morrow, Mr. *Rust.*

Rust. I thank you, my good Friend; have you visited your Wards this Morning? Are all Things safe, ha?

Care. Ay, ay, there's nothing out of Order, I promise you, except it be my Head, for it akes consumedly. I made a little too bold with my Constitution last Night; but who can avoid Drinking, when there comes such a Glut of Company to see this Fellow, this *Sheppard?* To tell you the Truth, Master *Rust,* he's worth very much to us; and I believe will turn to a good Account.

Rust. Hist, hist, he's pretty well. Don't speak your Mind too freely; you and I know

B   the

33

(2)

the Sweets of taking Money, and so does our Master, the Governor of this enchanted Castle: But let's not blab, let us be merry and wise, good Mr. *Careful*.

Care. I hope we shan't lose him again. I'd have him hang'd as soon, methinks——

Rust. No, no, they can't hang him but according to the Rules of Law; and tho' he be dead in Law, yet we must prove him to be the individual, numerical, identical living Person, that was condemn'd by the Name of *John Sheppard*; which can't be done till next Sessions.

Care. While we, in the mean time, reap the Advantage of him.

Rust. Right, and it stands us upon to be tender of him: Or if he shou'd slip away again, which indeed, I think impossible, 'tis but like a Mouse getting free from a Cat; if we don't immediately recover him, we are sure he'll be our Prey one time or another.

Care. But if he's hang'd once, then——

Rust. Ay, then farewell to him, and the Profits arising from him. No, hang him, I wou'd not have him hang'd yet. But here's Company coming; some Fools who are curious to see a dextrous Knave; tho' I think 'tis a little too early in the Morning to have Visiters. Who is it, Mr. *Careful?*

Care.

(3)

Care. Our best Friend, our *Primum Mobile*, that sets all our Springs a going. *Jonathan Wile*.

Rust. You are happy in a choice Phrase. *Primum Mobile* is very pretty. But, Mr. *Careful*, I allow no Servant of the Goal to speak *Latin*. Suppose we had any *Jesuits* here now, as Pris'ners, you might be suspected to carry on a clandestine Correspondence with 'em.

Care. Well, well, I stand Corrected.

Rust. Now I have a Right to speak *Latin*, 'tis as necessary for a Master Goaler to be a Linguist, as to be a Lawyer; and I am as good a Lawyer as any that ply at the *Old-Baily*. Nay, I'm as good a Lawyer as I am a Linguist. I have had more Experience I'm sure than half of 'em. But why does not Mr. *Wile* come in?

Care. He's gone to give *Blueskin* a Quartern of *Geneva*.

Rust. Has *Blueskin* any Weapon about him? For if he has, he may cut poor *Jonathan*'s Throat again.

Care. Why if he does, 'tis but Life for Life.

Rust. Ay, but Brother *Careful*, we must not lose *Jonathan*.

Enter Jonathan.

Jon. Lose *Jonathan!* No, my Buffs, he's worth twenty lost Persons yet. Tho' the

B 2 Dog

---

1. *Primum Mobile:* first mover
2. *Old-Baily:* London criminal court
3. *Blueskin:* see headnote to *Harlequin Sheppard*
4. Quartern: the fourth part of a pint
5. *Geneva:* gin
6. Buffs: fellows

34

(4)

7 Dog has fmach'd me damnably. But 'tis better to bear this Mark, than one made by a Halter, as that Rogue *Blueskin* foon will. Well, and how does *Sheppard!* Have you feen him to Day?

Care. Not yet.

Jon. Well, when you fee him, remember my Love to him. I can't ftay with you now, for I muft go and drink with the Fellows I condemn'd laft Seffions, they dye to Morrow. And you know old Friends muft part as Friends.

Ruft. You are very kind to 'em, Mr. *Wile.*

Jon. Ay, fo you'd fay, if you knew all.
8 I'll engage it cofts me a Crown at leaft, every Execution Day, in treating one or another of 'em. Befides the Lofs of my Time,
9 attending 'em at the Tree: For I love to fee the laft of 'em. Well, I fhall fend you in half a dozen Fellows by and by. I have a dead Set upon the Rogues. See, I'm in order and prepar'd for 'em. My old Piftols that I took from *Spiggot*, fee, and my Favourite here, the *Arm-pit* Piftol. Oh! this dear little Rogue, he makes my Pot boil. He does more Execution than a great Cannon.

Care. That will demolifh a Thief as foon as you can take an Oath; and that's pretty expeditious.

Jon.

7. fmach'd: fmacked, ftruck
8. Crown: a coin worth five fhillings
9. the Tree: the gallows, 'Tyburn Tree'

(5)

Jon. Well, get your Lodgings in Order, againft Night, for your new Comers.

Ruft. Mr. *Wile,* I fancy you had better let alone taking of 'em, till to Morrow, becaufe we are ftraiten'd for Room in the 10 Goal, but to Morrow being Execution Day, we can difpofe of 'em more conveniently.

Jon. Pfha, pfha, if you have not Beds for 'em, put them among the condemn'd Thieves for one Night, I'll engage they won't quarrel among themfelves. Fare you well. I wifh you as good a Day as you had Yefterday. [*Exit.*

Care. Well, I'll fay that for my Friend *Jonathan,* he's a careful, diligent Soul; he does not meet tho' with half that Encouragement from the Government he does from us; 'tis pity.

Ruft. Ah, Brother *Careful,* you look thro' the wrong End of the Perfpective at 11 Things. *Jonathan* is very well in his Way; but I have heard fome Thieves, ay, and honeft People too, fay, he deferves hanging as much as *Sheppard.* But he's our Friend, and I won't rail at him too much. Who comes here?

Enter a Gentleman.

Gent. I have a Defire, Gentlemen, to fee this famous *Sheppard,* and if you'll gratify me, 'twill oblige me.

Ruft.

10. ftraiten'd: in difficulty
11. Perfpective: an optical glafs, as a telefcope

35

II. The Underworld Background

Unless we recapture the reverberations of "Newgate," the setting for nearly half the *Opera*, we will fail to see how violently paradoxical Gay's romanticism is. A rough equivalent today would be writing a musical comedy about an American penitentiary. Lockit's Newgate seems a picturesque and pleasant enough place, where Lucys help their handsome lovers escape and everyone breaks regularly into song. What theatre-goers silently supplied, we may suppose, was a knowledge of Newgate's squalor, jail-fever, intolerable promiscuity, drunkenness, and for the poor, near or actual starvation.

John Howard, the great philanthropist, in his *The State of the Prisons in England and Wales* (1777), remarks on the "malignity" of the air in the prisons he visited, 'My cloaths were in my first journeys so offensive, that in a post-chaise I could not bear the windows drawn up; and was therefore often obliged to travel on horseback. The leaves of my memorandum-book were often so tainted, that I could not use it till after spreading it an hour or two before the fire: and even my antidote, a vial of vinegar, has after using it in a few prisons, become intolerably disagreeable" (p.13). Contemporary accounts of Newgate are less sober and detailed than one could wish, but the excerpt we print from *The History Of The Press-Yard* gives some of their flavor.

A few facts may be helpful. Prisons in the early part of the eighteenth century (there were about 150 in London) were typically divided into "sides" or "Wards," and the prisoner was placed in the one he could afford. Each prison usually (there were, of course, many variations) had a Master's Ward, a Knight's Ward, a Two-penny Ward, and a Common Ward. The Press Yard was an open space, appended to the Master's Ward, where the wealthier prisoners could take exercise. Newgate had some special features: a sixty-foot tower that had several strong-rooms for the detention of particularly dangerous criminals (Jack Sheppard's most memorable escape was from one of these rooms), and the infamous Press Room where heavy weights were placed on prisoners who would not enter a plea in court. (A prisoner might refuse to enter a plea of guilty or not-guilty to prevent his captors from confiscating his belongings.) This torture was legal and could be continued until the prisoner entered a plea—or died.

The most comfortable Side was the Master's Side where the prisoner usually had his own cell and any furniture he wanted to bring in. It has been calculated that a room here, plus privileges in the Press Yard, cost up to £500 as a deposit, and 22s. a week rent. By today's standards that comes to about £10,000 deposit and £22 rent for one small room.[1] The alternative must have made it worth the money. In the Common Side prisoners are described as living "far worse than swine," in danger of becoming "poisoned with their own filth" (*An Accurate Description of Newgate*, 1724, p.45). An even more gruesome part of the Common Ward was the Stone Hold (where Jack Sheppard was incarcerated after one of his escapes). Prisoners here lived in freezing cold, total darkness, and filth, since no consistent plan was in effect for the removal of excrement. Those who were unable to pay their fees were crowded into this cave and were entirely dependent for their food upon the charity of the gaolers.

When a man was arrested by the Sheriff or his officers and taken to Newgate, the first thing he had to do was pay his fees, according to an official scale. The prisoner unable to pay anything was thrown into the Stone Hold and kept there until he could pay the 2s.6d fee for entry into the Common Ward (*History Of The Press-Yard*, p.47). Once the fees were settled with the turnkey, the prisoner would be taken to the Lodge, a sort of pub where he could buy tobacco, beer, wine, and spirits. Once in the Side he had to pay the Steward, usually the oldest prisoner there, "garnish money"; in 1724 this would have been 10s.6d. With the garnish money drinks were ordered from the Lodge for all the inmates of the Side. Often the

---

1. Gerald Howson, *Thief-Taker General, The Rise and Fall of Jonathan Wild* (London: Hutchinson, 1970), pp.28.

prisoner who had no money was stripped and his clothes sold for liquor.

The garnish Lockit demands of Macheath in II.vii. for lighter chains was perfectly legal, and as principal gaoler of Newgate he had a right to the money. Any Lockit had to obtain his position from the Crown, through bidding in auction, the person with the highest bid being granted the right of sole concession. To get his money back then, he extorted fees and garnish for liquor, food, walking space, lighter chains, and bedding. A final outrageous feature of this system forced prisoners acquitted of crimes to pay a discharge fee.

The History Of The Press Yard: Or, a Brief Account of the Customs and
Occurrences that are put in Practice, and to be met with in that Antient
Repository of Living Bodies, called, His Majesty's Goal of Newgate in
London . . . London, Printed for T. Moor in St. Paul's Church-yard,
1717. Pp. 4-7. The first chapter complete.

C H A P. I.

Of the Author's Imprisonment, &c.

NOW it being my Misfortune, amongſt other Brethren of the Quill, to be caught Tripping, in Cenſuring the Conduct of my Superiors, and to fall under the Diſpleaſure of the Government, for pretending to be diſpleas'd at their Proceedings, I was judg'd ſo little worthy of being maintain'd at *6 s.* and **8** *d. per* Day in the Meſſengers Hands at the King's Expence, That, after I had been indulg'd that Favour ſome Weeks, I was very decently Conducted in a Coach to the Place of my future Reſidence called *Newgate*, there to reflect with my ſelf on my paſt Indiſcretion, and to cool my Heels, till the Act for ſuſpending the *Habeas Corpus* Act for a certain Time ſhould be out of Force. It is eaſie to be judg'd that my Countenance was none of the pleaſanteſt, when I found my ſelf in the Lodge, encompaſs'd by a parcel of ill-look'd Fellows, that ey'd me, as if they would look me through, and examin'd every part of me from Head to Toe, not as Taylours to take Meaſure of me, but as Foot-Pads that Survey the goodneſs of the Clothes firſt, before they grow intimate with the Linings, and uncaſe the Travellers from the Incumbrance of them.

Quoth

---

1. Messengers Hands: Press Messengers were a police force whose duty it was to hunt out authors of treasonable literature. Our author had been in a private prison before being sent to Newgate.
2. Foot-Pads: highwaymen who rob on foot

Quoth a Fellow with the moſt rueful
Appearance that ever Creature with two
Legs ever made, to his Doxy, that I under- 3
ſtood was a Runner upon all Neceſſary oc-
caſions of the Goal, *DOL, We ſhall have a*
Hot Supper to Night, the Cull looks as if he 4
had the Blunt, and I muſt come in for a ſhare 5
of it , after my few Maſters have done with
him, and began to Rattle a Bunch of Keys
in his Hand, to call for Half a Pint of
Brandy to drink his new Maſter's Health;
which was immediately brought by a ſhort
thick Protuberance of Female Fleſh, not leſs
than five Yards in the Waſt, and ſent down
Gutter-Lane inſtantly (as well it might) 6
being little more than the quantity of Half
a Quartern. Madam, ſaid I to her, for I 7
found the Beaſt had that Appellation given
to her, Which are the Perſons that are to
take care of me? *Bring the Gentleman a Flaſk*
of the beſt Claret, that which Mr. Kent *ſent in*
laſt, quick, quick, Sirrah, was all the Anſwer I could have from her. Whereupon
I repeated my Queſtion, and deſired her to
pledge me, which ſhe did in a Bumper,
and reply'd, *A Bottle of* French *White for*
the Gentleman. You ſhall have it, Sir, as
good as any in England, *take the Word of an*
honeſt Woman for it. Now this *Honeſt Wo-*
man, as I was afterwards told, was an old
Convicted Offender, one that had gone
through every Degree of Iniquity, and by
receiving Sentence of Death for the ſame,
was

---

3. Doxy: mistress, prostitute
4. *Cull:* dupe, fool
5. *Blunt:* ready money
6. Gutter-Lane: the throat
7. Quartern: the fourth part of a pint

was arriv'd at the Zenith of Perfection in that Art and Miſtery. Heavens, cry'd I to my ſelf, *How juſtly am I puniſh'd for the Sins of my Youth, in this Execrable Converſation!* while all Hands were at Work in putting the Glaſs round, for the good of the Houſe, as they call'd it, and ſix or ſeven Flasks were conſumed after this manner, and the value of as much more in Brandy, which was all paid down upon the Nail for, before I could get the Woman, or Monſter above mention'd, to tell me what Appartment I was to have my Abode in ; and then ſhe took upon her to whiſper me, and ſay, *Dear Sir, you ſeem to be a very Civil Gentleman, and will no doubt be Treated*
8 *as ſuch by Mr. R——ſe, and Mr. R——l, who know how to diſtinguiſh Perſons of Worth from Soundrels.* I gave her a Hearing, and thank'd her with a Bow, but neither of thoſe Men of Compaſſion at that juncture came near me.

In the mean time this pair of Irons, and that pair of Fetters, were handed about from one to the other behind me, and I had the mortification of being Terrified with, *a Pair of Forty Pounds Weight will be enough for him,* ſpoke by way of Wiſper, *We ought to ſend to the Governour to know whether he is to be Hand-Cuff'd.* This made me ready to enter into a Treaty by way of Prevention, and again to enquire for the Perſons who had Authority to manage it, which one or
two

---

8. R_ſe, R_l: unidentified. R_ſe is perhaps the keeper mentioned on p. 17 of Defoe's *Narrative*. See below, p. 61.

two lly Thieves about me, laying hold of, infinuated to me that it was in their Power to make an Intereft as to my Irons, and that upon fuch and fuch Confiderations they would ferve me. Hereupon I, without any Hefitation, thruft the Purport of their Argument into their Hands, but found it very indifferently beftow'd from the Confequence of it; for inftead of a Handfome Appartment which I was made to hope for through their fuggeftions, after I had been cajol'd into a Belief of all poffible Civilities, by my Fat Tunbellied Hoftefs, who applauded me for the Tallnefs of my fhape, that bore a great Refemblance to that of a late humble Servant of hers, I was conducted to the Door leading out of the Lodge into the Condemn'd Hold, where they told me I muft ftay till their Mafters further Pleafure fhould be known, for they could go no further than the eafing me of Irons, which they did not know but they might have Anger for, by Reafon of the Capitalnefs of the Crime whereof I ftood accus'd.

---

9. Tunbellied: pot-bellied
10. Condemn'd Hold: the Stone Hold; see introduction to this chapter

The Beggar's Opera is tied to Newgate by more than its setting. In broad fashion, Peachum and Macheath are drawn after the two best known criminals of the eighteenth century—Jonathan Wild and John Sheppard. Peachum, the thief-taker and dealer in stolen goods, resembles Wild in his activities; Macheath, the romantic hero, resembles Sheppard, especially in his escapes from Newgate.

By 1719 Jonathan Wild had achieved his greatest power. His gang controlled nearly all of the underworld activity in London. He was also "Thief-Taker General," a highly profitable business. Through a systematic and ruthless betrayal of criminals, he had not only fragmented other gangs but held his own men in absolute control. A thief-taker, according to the Highwayman Act of 1693, received a forty-pound reward for arresting a thief and bringing evidence against him that would lead to a conviction. Those Wild turned in usually were members of his gang of thieves who were not productive enough or else were caught concealing their booty from him. Some of the early scenes in *The Beggar's Opera* show Peachum deciding who will be turned over to the law and who has been a productive member of his gang. Wild's near monopoly on London crime made it possible for him to engage in his other most famous activity

—the return of stolen goods to the rightful owner for a suitable fee. Peachum, too, undertakes to render this service (I.viii.). Wild (like Peachum) was pretty certain to know who had committed the robbery and where the stolen goods were; Wild had several warehouses for receiving and hiding stolen goods; Peachum had one at Redriff (I.vi.). By the early 1720s Wild was so much a part of the establishment that he could, with impunity, advertise his services, the recovery of stolen goods, in *The Daily Post*.

Wild's luck finally began to run out. New legislation made it a felony for a person to take money or a reward for recovering stolen goods, the punishment to be the same as for the original theft. Finally members of his gang betrayed him and he was arrested in 1725, convicted of taking £10 as a reward for returning stolen property, and executed 24 May 1725.

We reprint first a tantalizing anecdote of a meeting between Gay and Wild which just might be true, although if it is, it is odd that Pope never told Spence about it. Next, after several of Wild's advertisements, we reprint an excerpt from one of the popular lives of Wild. *Mist's Weekly Journal*, 22 May 1725, gives in eleven points a clear summary of Wild's startling career.

from *The Flying-Post*, 11 January, 1729.

An friend of an eminent poet, has sent us the following account of the circumstance which gave the first hint to the celebrated English Opera, *that gave the kingdom so much diversion last winter, and is now acted by* Pigmies. *The author, and a friend of his, being at an instalment at* Windsor, *could not get a room for themselves in the whole town, but at last kind fate directed their steps to a place, where a gentleman was alone, and waiting for some company; upon their desire to be admitted, the gentleman sent word that the room was at their service, and accordingly they were introduc'd. After they had talk'd together for some time, they found they were got with the genuine* Peachum, (*executed a few years ago*) *who discours'd with great freedom on his profession, and set it in such a light, that the poet imagin'd he might work up the incidents of it for the stage; and in order to make Mr.* Peachum *reveal the mysteries of his art, he ply'd him lustily with wine, and pretended that both he and his companion, were upon the same expedition with himself, but that they had no associates. The poet, who continued to personate a—, and had several interviews afterwards with Mr.* Peachum, *and*

some say, brought him some things, which he pretended to have got by slight of hand. By his great familiarity with him, he let him into all the knavish offices and intrigues of the thieving trade ; and the great and good use, that was made of them, is too well known to the public, to be mention'd in this place.

---

1. an instalment at Windsor: an Instalment of Knights of the Garter, 1 August 1724, in ceremonies at Windsor, where Wild was supervising robberies
2. a—; a thief

Samples of advertisements Wild placed in *The Daily Post*

The Daily Post, 13 February 1724.

Lost on Sunday Night the 9th Instant, about 7 in the evening, off of a Horses Back, between the King's Head in the Borough and Temple Bar, a Portmanteau Trunk, with a Livery Coat, Frock and Breeches, with other wearing Apparrel, besides several papers. Whoever will bring the same to Mr. Jonath. Wilde in the Old Baily,[1] shall have 4 Guineas[2] Reward, or whoever will discover the person concerned in the said Robbery, so that he may be brought to Justice, will have the same Reward.

The Daily Post, 26 March 1724.

Lost on Saturday Night a Packet, being torn from a woman in Cornhill, in the narrow passage going into the Jamaica Coffee-house, in which was a Diamond Ring in a Shagreen[3] Case, in a green and white Purse, a laced Handerchief, and a Silver Snuff Box with a Cypher[4] on it, a Pair of Silver Buckles, some Money, and a Key. If any person will bring the aforesaid Things to Mr. Jonathan Wild in the Old Baily, shall receive 4 guineas Reward; or whosoever will discover the person or persons concern'd in the said Robbery, shall have 5 guineas Reward for such Discovery paid by the said Johnathan Wild.

The Daily Post, 5 June 1724.

Whereas there was stolen out of the Vine-Inn in Bishops-gate-street, on Monday Night last, out of two Boxes, several Goods; if any of the Persons concern'd therein, can discover who committed the Fact, so as they may be apprehended, and convicted, upon applying to Mr. Jonathan Wild in the Old Baily, they shall be admitted as Evidence, and receive 3 guineas.

---

1. Wild lived at 68 Old Bailey, near the criminal court
2. an English coin worth 21 shillings
3. a kind of untanned leather, frequently dyed green
4. monogram

The Life And Glorious Actions Of the most Heroic and Magnanimous Jonathan Wilde . . . London: Printed for H. Whitridge, in Searle-street by Lincolns-Inn Back-Gate. 1725. Pp. 49-54.

Profecution, and to give him up his Inden-
ture, and difcharge him; which accordingly was done ; to the great damage and total ruin of fome Hundreds fince.

Jonathan   .   .   .   imme-
diately repair'd to his Companions in *Drury-* 1
lane, where for a long time he continued,
and at length was almoft ftarved to Death
(for you muft underftand that, at that time,
that Trade of *Drury-lane* was very dull,
and therefore he was glad to take up with
his old Trade of being a Setter to a Marfhal's 2
Court Bailiff, which he practis'd in the Day
time, and at Night to be a Bully, and herein he got his living as moft Irifh-men do, at
their firft coming into *England,* viz. By
cowardly taking Men by the Backs, and
impudently taking Women by the Bellies,
and after that fet up for Stallions. By that
time three Years of this living had pafs'd o-
ver his head, he began to have a great acquaintance amongft the moft reputed Bawds
and common Whores ; and at laft, according to the Cuftom of the *Fleet,* was mar- 3
ried to an old Bawd, who was alfo what the
Thieves call a *Fencer, viz.* a Receiver of
ftolen Goods from Thieves : And here began
the firft rife of Honeft *Jonathan's* late Pro-
G   feffion

---

1. *Drury-Lane*: famous for its prostitutes
2. Setter to a Marshal's Court Bailiff: a setter is a police spy; the Upper Marshall and
   the Under Marshall and their men—here, bailiffs—were a private police force
   of the Court of Alderman of the City. In reality, Wild had been a setter to some
   bailiffs attached to the Marshalsea Court in Clifford's Inn, Holborn.
3. the *Fleet*: London prison, largely for debtors; 'Fleet marriages,' performed for a
   small fee by disreputable clergymen in the prison, were notorious.

feſſion or Practice of *Thief-taking*. When
two years more had paſs'd, his old Wife the
Mother of *Beelzebub,* took a leap in the
Dark and thereby Friend *Jonathan* became
a very good Bawdy Batchelour, (or as the
Old Women term it, a Young Widower.)
And as this Infernal Bawd had practis'd her
wicked ways of living for many Years, ſhe
had thereby acquired great ſtore of Plate,
Watches, Rings, *&c.* which *Honeſt Jona-
than* ſoon Metamorphized into the Sterling
Coin of *England.*

And as this Mother of Sin had been a
long and great encourager to Thieves, ſhe
had attracted a Company of near Fifteen
Hundred, compoſed of Men, Women and
Children , with whom *Honeſt Jonathan*
Articled, That on condition they gave him
all the Things they Stole, he would pay
them one half of the value thereof, and be
4 true to them, without Whidling, and alſo
provide and aſſiſt them with Money, at ſuch
Times when they were obliged to beat the
ſame March, *viz.* at ſuch time when they
had no Money, and could not light of a
Prize; and to ſupply them with proper In-
ſtruments for their purpoſe when required.
And as the number of them were very nu—
merous

---

4. Whidling: to whiddle or whidle is to turn informer, 'peach'

merous, He therefore divided them into
several Companies, in such a manner as he
thought most convenient . . . . . .

. . . .

. . . .

. . . .

. . . .

. . . .

. . . .

And to each Company he assign'd certain Walks or Places, wherein they should
Rob, and also appointed a Governour of
each Company under him, who twice in
every Week was oblig'd to attend him,
and bring their plunder, to whom was paid,
as before agreed on, which this Sub-Governour distributed equally amongst those of
his Company.

And at those times of these Sub-Governours attending him, he always appointed
fresh Walks to every Company, the better
to prevent notice being taken of them by
a long Duration in one Place.

G 2

He

He alſo at every Attendance given him
by thoſe Sub-Governours, inquires who performed beſt, and who not; which being
anſwer'd, he forthwith gives Commiſſion
to the Sub-Governour to introduce them as
are incapable into ſome Robbery, wherein
one or the other as is moſt polite ſhall ſuf-
fer himſelf to be taken, on purpoſe to make
himſelf an Evidence againſt them, and for
ſo doing is allowed one fifth part of the
Reward given by the Government (to *Ho-*
neſt Jonathan, who apprehends them) for
every one that is Convicted; ſo that 'tis
demonſtrable, that whoſoever of thoſe Thick-
Headed Rouges can't bring Griſt to his Mill,
5, 6 muſt expect to be *Nubb'd*, by *Quilting Ar-*
7 *nol* at the *Nubbing Cheat*.

And to prevent thoſe Governours from
diſcovering his dealing with them, he generally
every other Seſſions cauſes one or two to
be Hang'd out of the way, and thereby the
others are deterr'd.

Theſe Governours, at their Attendance
twice in every Week, was obliged to give
an account in what manner, and from whom,
the Goods where ſtolen from and thereby he
knew how to give Information of the ſame,
and proceed againſt them as he thought proper.   And

---

5. *Nubb'd*: hanged
6. *Quilting Arnold*: Quilt Arnold, one of Wild's chief assistants; to 'quilt' is to beat
   or flog
7. *Nubbing Cheat*: the gallows

And finding that his Number greatly en-creafed, to prevent Difcoveries by the old ones, he was obliged to hang them out of the way, which put him in fuch a hurry that he was obliged to leave his Dwelling in *Drury-lane,* and take another near to the *Seffions Houfe* in the *Old Baily,* that he might always be at hand at every Call when occafions required.

By fuch time as Eleven Years had pafs'd over his Head, in this wicked Courfe of Life, by his Hanging of many Hundreds of Theives, he acquired the Title of *Thief-taker,* or *Thief-catcher,* and there-upon fuch Perfons apply'd to him, as had been robb'd by his Emiffaries, to know whe-ther he could help them to their Goods, *&c.* ftoln, upon the payment of fuch a Sum as would fatisfie the appetite of this Mon-ftrous Beaft.

The Reward being thus agreed on, *Ho-neft Jonathan* repairs to his Day Book, and examines what Company was on that Walk, where the Robbery was committed, and thereby knowing the Governour there-of, fends for him, who forthwith produces the Goods ftoln, if not taken by Thieves as are not of their Tribe.

The Agreement made between this Honest Fellow, and thofe as have loft their Goods is at follows. If your Goods is to be heard on, at any Pawn-brokers, &c. Upon the Payment of - - - - - - - at the Sign of the - - - - - - - in - - - - - - - They fhall be inclofed in a Hamper, Cask, &c. and juftly deliver'd to any Perfon upon the Payment of the Money - - - - And then he appoints a Day for the fame. And in the mean time, if the Goods are ftoln by his Emiffaries and the Reward fufficient, they are convey'd to the place affign'd, where, upon Payment of the Money agreed on (which is always paid in Difcharge of a Conditional Indemnifying Note) the Hamper-Cask, &c. is deliver'd, and no Queftions asked.

from Mist's Weekly Journal, 22 May 1725

The Seffions concluded that Evening, and there received Sentence of Death five Perfons, viz. Jonathan Wild, Robert Harpam, John Plant, William Sperry and Robert Sandford ; the two laft for Robberies on the Highway, and Plant for a Street Robbery.

Mr. Serjeant Baynes, and Mr. Kettleby, appeared as Council for Jonathan Wild, and Mr. Attorney General for his Majefty. At his receiving Sentence, he acknowledged his Guilt of the Fact, and the frequent Admonitions given him by Mr. Recorder, to avoid fuch Practices ; pleaded his Services in apprehending of Robbers, and begg'd for Tranfportation.

John Cooper, alias Blind Cooper, was convicted of a Mifdemeanor, in uttering counterfeit Money knowingly, for which Offence he was fin'd 100 l. and a Year's Imprifonment.

Quilt Arnold, Wild's Man, who was taken up with his Mafter, is order'd to remain till the enfuing Affizes for Effex, when he is to be remov'd thither to be try'd for a capital Crime charged upon him in that County.

On Wednefday the Dead Warrant came down to Newgate for the Execution of four of the abovefaid Malefactors on Monday next at Tyburn, viz. Jonathan Wild, Robert Harpam, William Sperry and Robert Sanford ; John Plant is repriev'd.

Jonathan is attended in the Condemn'd Hold by the Reverend Mr. Nicholfon, Lecturer of St. Sepulchres, to prepare him for his approaching Change. He is, as yet, under the greateft Horrors and Agonies of Mind ; which, 'tis hop'd may work a good Effect for the fhort Time he has to live, as well upon his wicked Companions as himfelf.

As there are many confiderable Bleffings derived to the People of this Nation, from the excellent Nature of its Government ; fo none of them is more to be valued and admired than the impartial and merciful Method prefcribed by our Laws and Courts of Juftice, in their Proceedings againft common Offenders wherein the leaft Attempt to prepoffefs, or biafs any of the Judges, or Jury, is punifhed as highly Criminal.

This is the Reafon why the publick hath not hitherto had a more certain Account than has yet been printed of *Jonathan Wild's* Practices, who being now under Sentence of Death, can receive no Prejudice by the Publication of this Abftract of Informations that have been made againft him upon Oath ; by which it will appear, how neceffary it was for the common Safety of Mankind to bring him to Juftice.

1. It appears by feveral Informations upon Oath, that Jonathan Wild hath, for many Years paft, been a Confederate with great Numbers of Highwaymen, Pick-pockets, Houfe-breakers, Shoplifters, and other Thieves.

2. That he hath form'd a kind of Corporation of Thieves, of which he is the Head or Director, and that notwithftanding his pretended Services in detecting and profecuting Offenders, he procured fuch only to be hang'd as conceal'd their Booty or refufed to fhare it with him.

3. That he hath divided the Town and Country into fo many Diftricts, and appointed diftinct Gangs for each, who regularly accounted with him for their Robberies. He had alfo a particular Set to fteal at Churches in Time of divine Service, and alfo other moving Detachments to attend at Court on Birth-Days, Balls, &c. and upon both Houfes of Parliament, Circuits, and Country Fairs.

4. That the Perfons employ'd by him were for the moft part Felons Convict, who have return'd from Tranfportation before the Time for which they were tranfported was expired, and that he made Choice of them to be his Agents, becaufe they could not be legal Evidence againft him, and becaufe he had it in his Power to take from them what Part of the ftolen Goods he thought fit, and otherwife ufe them ill, or hang them, as he pleafed.

5. That he hath from Time to Time fupplied fuch convicted Felons with Money and Cloaths, and lodged them in his own Houfe, the better to conceal them, particularly fome againft whom there are now Informations for diminifhing and counterfeiting Broad-Pieces and Guineas.[1]

6. That he hath not only been a Receiver of ftolen Goods, as well as of Writings of all Kinds for near fifteen Years laft paft, but frequently been a Confederate, and robb'd along with the abovementioned convicted Felons.

7. That in order to carry on thefe vile Practifes to gain fome Credit with the ignorant Multitude, he ufually carried about him a fhort Silver Staff, as a Badge of Authority from the Government, which he ufed to produce when he himfelf was concerned in robbing.

8. That he had under his Care and Direction feveral Warehoufes for receiving and concealing ftolen Goods ; and alfo a Ship for carrying off Jewels, Watches, and other valuable Goods to Holland, where he hath a fuperannuated Thief for his Factor.[2]

9. That he kept in Pay feveral Artifts to make Alterations, and transform Watches, Seals, Snuff-Boxes, Rings, and other valuable Things, that they might not be known, feveral of which he ufed to prefent to fuch Perfons as he thought might be of Service to him.

10. That he feldom or ever helped the Owners to their Notes and Papers they had loft, unlefs he found them able exactly to fpecify and defcribe them, and then often infifted on more than half the Value.

11. Laftly, it appears that he hath frequently fold human Blood, by procuring falfe Evidence to fwear Perfons into Facts they were not guilty of, fometimes to prevent them from being Evidence againft himfelf ; at others, for the fake of the great Reward given by the Government.

---

1. Broad-Pieces and Guineas: coins worth respectively 20 and 21 shillings.
2. Factor: agent

Wild's counterpart in crime and infamy was Jack Sheppard, whose career was more or less concurrent with Wild's. Sheppard and his gang were related to Wild's gang in much the same way as Macheath is related to Peachum (see II.ii). Sheppard was a great womanizer, and in one of his escapes was aided by Elizabeth Lyon; Macheath in his escape is aided by Lucy Lockit. Some time after this, Elizabeth betrayed Sheppard to Wild; just so Mrs. Trapes betrays Macheath.

Sheppard was imprisoned in the strongest room of Newgate, called "The Castle." Loaded with padlocks and chains, he escaped through the rooms of the Gate Tower, having succeeded in breaking down six iron doors, with make-shift tools, in total darkness. On reaching the tower, he discovered he had to go back for a blanket in order to make his descent to the roof of a neighbouring house, and so into the street. He was immediately a hero. When he was finally recaptured and convicted, his execution drew a crowd of two hundred thousand people. Defoe's not always accurate biography, which appeared the day after Sheppard's execution, laid the groundwork for the romantic hero Sheppard was to become in the character of Macheath. We reprint an excerpt from Defoe's tract, together with "An Epistle from Jack Sheppard," which (much like Gay), finds Wild's and Sheppard's judges as corrupt as those they judge.

[Daniel Defoe]. A Narrative Of all the Robberies, Escapes, &c. Of John Sheppard . . . London: Printed and Sold by John Applebee, a little below Bridewell-Bridge, in Black-Fryers. 1974. Pp. 13-23.

ry fent me to St. *Giles*'s Round-houfe for
that Night, with Orders to the Conftable
to bring me before him again the next Morning for farther Examination. I had nothing but an old Razor in my Pocket, and
was confin'd in the upper Part of the Place,
being two Stories from the Ground; with
my Razor I cut out the Stretcher of a
Chair, and began to make a Breach in the
Roof, laying the Feather-bed under it to
prevent any Noife by the falling of the
Rubbifh on the Floor. It being about nine at
Night, People were paffing and repaffing in
the Street, and a Tile or Brick happening to
fall, ftruck a Man on the Head, who rais'd
the whole Place; the People calling aloud
that the Prifoners were breaking out of
the Round-houfe. I found there was no
Time then to be loft, therefore made a
bold Pufh thro' the Breach, throwing a
whole Load of Bricks, Tiles, &c. upon
the People in the Street; and before the
Beadle and Affiftance came up I had dropt
into the Church-yard, and got over the
lower End of the Wall, and came amidft
the Crowd, who were all ftaring up, fome
crying, *there's his Head, there he goes behind the Chimney*, &c. I was well enough
diverted with the Adventure, and then
went off about my Bufinefs.

The Methods by which I efcap'd from
New-Prifon, and the *Condemn'd Hold* of
Newgate,

Newgate, have been printed in fo many Books and Papers, that it would be ridiculous to repeat them ; only it muſt be remember'd that my Eſcaping from *New-*
1 *Priſon,* and carrying wi:h me *Elizabeth*
2 *Lyon* over the Wall of *Bridewell* Yard, was not fo wonderful as has been reported, becauſe
3 Captain *Geary* and his Servants cannot but know, that by my opening the great Gate I got *Lyon* upon the Top cf the Wall without the Help of a ſcaliug Ladder, otherwiſe it muſt have been impracticable to have procur'd her Redemption. She indeed rewarded me as well for it, in betraying me to *Jonathan Wild* fo foon after. I wiſh ſhe may reform her Life : a more wicked, deceitful and laſcivious Wretch there is not living in *England.* She has prov'd my Bane. God forgive her : I do ; and die in Charity with all the reſt of Mankind.

4   *Blueskin* has atton'd for his Offences. I am now following, being juſt on the Brink of Eternity, much unprepar'd to appear before the Face of an angry God. *Blueskin* had been a much older Offender than my ſe'f, having been guilty of numberleſs Robberies, and had formerly Convicted four of his Accomplices, who were put to Death. He was concern'd along with me in the three Robberies on the *Hampſtead* Road, beſides that of Mr. *Kneebone,* and one other.

---

1. *Elizabeth Lyon:* Sheppard's companion, known as 'Edgworth Bess,' who betrayed him to Wild
2. *Bridewell:* house of correction for prisoners; Clerkenwell Bridewell is meant here
3. Captain *Geary:* unidentified
4. *Blueskin:* see headnote to *Harlequin Sheppard*

ther. Tho' he was an able-bodied Man
and capable of any Crime, even Murder,
he was never Matter of a Courage or Conduct suitable to our Enterprizes; and I am
of Opinion, that neither of us had so soon
met our Fate, if he would have suffer'd himself to have been directed by me; he always wanting Resolution, when our Affairs
requir'd it most. The last Summer, I hired
two Horses for us at an Inn in *Piccadilly*,
and being arm'd with Pistols, &c. we went
upon *Enfield-Chace*, where a Coach pass'd
us with two Footmen and four young Ladies, who had with them their Gold Watches, Tweezer Cases and other things of
Value; I declar'd immediately for attack-
ing them, but *Blueskin*'s Courage dropt him,
saying that he would first refresh his Horse
and then follow, but he designedly delayed
till we had quite lost the Coach and Hopes of
the Booty. In short, he was a worthless
Companion, a sorry Thief, and nothing but
the cutting of *Jonathan Wild*'s Throat
could have made him so considerable.

I have often lamented the scandalous
Practice of Thief-catching, as it is call'd,
and the publick Manner of offering Rewards for stoln Goods, in Defiance of two
several Acts of Parliament; the Thief-Cat-
chers living sumptuously, and keeping of
publick Offices of Intelligence: these who
forfeit their Lives every Day they breathe,
and

and deferve the Gallows as richly as any of
the Thieves, fend us as their Reprefentatives
5 to *Tyburn* once a Month : thus they hang
by Proxy, while we do it fairly in Perfon.

I never correfponded with any of them.
I was indeed twice at a Thief-Catcher's
6 *Levee*, and muft confefs the Man treated
me civilly ; he complimented me on my
Succeffes, faid he heard that I had both an
Hand and Head admirably well turn'd to
Bufinefs, and that I and my Friends *fhould
be always welcome to him*: But caring not
for his Acquaintance, I never troubled him,
nor had we any Dealings together.

As my laft Efcape from *Newgate* out of
the ftrong Room call'd the *Caftle*, has made
a greater Noife in the World than any o-
ther Action of my Life, I fhall relate every minute Circumftance thereof as far as I
am able to remember: intending thereby
to fatisfie the Curious, and do Juftice to
the Innocent. After I had been made a
publick Spectacle for many Days together,
with my Legs chain'd together, loaded with
heavy Irons, and ftapled down to the Floor,
I thought it was not altogether impracticable to efcape, if I could but be furnifhed
with proper Implements ; but as every Perfon that came near me was carefully
watch'd, there was no Poffibility of any
fuch Affiftance ; till one Day in the Ab-
fence of my Jaylors, being looking about
the

---

5. *Tyburn*: the gallows
6. *Levee*: morning reception

the Floor, I fpy'd a fmall Nail within Reach, and with that, after a little Practice, I found the great Horfe Padlock that went from the Chain to the Staple in the Floor might be unlock'd, which I did afterward at pleafure; and was frequently about the Room, and have feveral times flept on the Barracks, when the Keepers imagin'd I had not been out of my Chair. But being unable to pafs up the Chimney, and void of Tools, I remain'd but where I was; till being detected in thefe Practices by the Keepers, who furpriz'd me one Day before I could fix my felf to the Staple in the manner as they had left me, I fhew'd Mr. *Pitt*, Mr. *Roufe*, 7 and Mr. *Parry* my Art, and before their Faces unlockt the Padlock with the Nail; and though People have made fuch an Outcry about it, there is fcarce a *Smith* in 8 *London* but what may eafily do the fame thing. However this call'd for a farther Security of me; and till now I had remain'd without Hand-Cuffs, and a jolly Pair was provided for me. Mr. *Kneebone* was prefent when they were put on: I with Tears begg'd his Interceffion to the Keepers to preferve me from thofe dreadful Manacles, telling him, my Heart was broken, and that I fhould be much more miferable than before. Mr. *Kneebone* could not refrain from fhedding Tears, and did ufe his good

C   Offices

7. Mr. *Pitt*, Mr. *Rouse*, Mr. *Parry*: unidentified. On Rouse, see above, p. 42.
8. *Smith*: locksmith

Offices with the Keepers to keep me from
them, but all to no purpose; on they went,
though at the same time I despis'd them,
and well knew that with my Teeth only I
could take them off at Pleasure: But this
was to lull them into a firm Belief, that they
had effectually frustrated all Attempts to escape for the future. I was still far from de-
spairing. The Turnkey and Mr. *Kneebone*
had not been gone down Stairs an Hour,
ere I made an Experiment, and got off my
Hand-Cuffs, and before they visited me a-
gain, I put them on, and industriously rubb'd
and fretted the Skin on my Wrists, making
them very bloody, as thinking (if such a
Thing was possible to be done) to move the
Turnkeys to Compassion, but rather to
confirm them in their Opinion; but though
this had no Effect upon them, it wrought
much upon the Spectators, and drew down
from them not only much Pity, but Quan-
9 tities of *Silver* and *Copper*: But I wanted
still a more useful *Metal,* a Crow, a Chissel,
a File, and a Saw or two, those Weapons
being more useful to me than all the Mines
of *Mexico*; but there was no expecting any
such Utensils in my Circumstances.

Wednesday the 14th of *October* the *Sessions* beginning, I found there was not a moment to be lost; and the Affair of *Jonathan
Wild*'s

9. *Silver* and *Copper:* coins

62

Wild's Throat, together with the Bufinefs at the *Old Baily*, having fufficiently engag'd 10 the Attention of the Keepers, I thought then was the Time to pufh. *Thurfday* the 15th at about two in the Afternoon *Auftin* my old Attendant came to bring my Neceffaries, and brought up four Perfons, *viz.* the Keeper of *Clerkenwell-Bridewell*, the 11 Clerk of *Weftminfter Gate-houfe*, and two others. *Auftin*, as it was his ufual Cuftom, examin'd the Irons and Hand-Cuffs, and found all fafe and firm, and then left me; and he may remember that I ask'd him to come again to me the fame Evening, but I neither expected or defired his Company; and happy was it for the poor Man that he did not interfere, while I had the large Iron Bar in my Hand, though I once had a Defign to have barricaded him, or any others from coming into the Room while I was at work; but then confidering that fuch a Project would be ufelefs, I let fall that Refolution.

As near as can be remember'd, juft before three in the Afternoon I went to work, taking off firft my Hand-Cuffs; next with main Strength I twifted a fmall Iron Link of the Chain between my Legs afunder; and the broken Pieces prov'd extream ufeful to me in my Defign; the Fett-Locks I drew 12 up to the Calves of my Leggs, taking off

C 2   before

---

10. *Old Baily*: the criminal court
11. *Clerkenwell-Bridewell, Westminster Gate-house*: London prisons
12. Fett-Locks: shackles for the legs

before that my Stockings, and with my Garters made them firm to my Body, to prevent their Shackling. I then proceeded to
make a Hole in the Chimney of the *Caftle*
about three Foot wide, and fix Foot high
from the Floor, and with the Help of the
broken Links aforefaid wrench'd an Iron
Bar out of the Chimney, of about two Feet
and an half in length, and an Inch fquare: a
moft notable Implement. I immediately enter'd the *Red Room* directly over the Caftle,
13 where fome of the *Prefton Rebels* had been
kept a long time agone ; and as the Keepers fay the Door had not been unlock'd for
feven Years; but I intended not to be feven
Years in opening it, though they had: I
went to work upon the Nut of the Lock,
and with little Difficulty got it off, and made
the Door fly before me ; in this Room I
found a large Nail, which prov'd of great
Ufe in my farther Progrefs. The Door of
the Entry between the *Red Room* and the
Chapel prov'd an hard Task, it being a la-
borious Piece of Work ; for here I was forc'd
to break away the Wall, and diflodge the
Bolt which was faften'd on the other Side.
This occafion'd much Noife, and I was very
14 fearful of being heard by the Mafter-Side
Debtors. Being got to the Chapel, I climb'd
over the Iron Spikes, and with Eafe broke
one of them off for my further Purpofes,
and

13. *Preston Rebels*: prisoners taken after the battle of Preston, August 1648, the final
    defeat of Charles I's Scottish supporters
14. Master-Side: see introduction to this chapter

and open'd the Door on the Infide. The
Door going out of the Chapel to the Leads, 15
I ftripp'd the Nut from off the Lock, as I
had done before from that of the *Red Room*,
and then got into the Entry between the
Chapel and the Leads; and came to another ftrong Door, which being faften'd by
a very ftrong Lock, there I had like to have
ftopt, and it being full dark, my Spirits began to fail me, as greatly doubting of fuc-
ceeding; but cheering up, I wrought on
with great Diligence, and in lefs than half
an Hour, with the main Help of the Nail
from the Red Room, and the Spike from
the Chapel, wrench'd the Box off, and fo
made the Door my Humble Servan..

A little farther in my Paffage another
ftout Door ftood in my Way; and this was
a Difficulty with a Witnefs; being guarded
with more Bolts, Bars, and Locks than any
I had hitherto met with: I had by this time
great Encouragement, as hoping foon to be
rewarded for all this Toil and Labour. The
Chimes at St. *Sepulchre*'s were now going the eighth Hour, and this prov'd a
very ufeful Hint to me foon after. I went
firft upon the Box and the Nut, but found
it Labour in vain; and then proceeded to
attack the Fillet of the Door; this fucceed- 16
ed beyond Expeftation, for the Box of the
Lock

---

15. Leads: lead roof
16. Fillet: 'a narrow strip of wood fastened upon any surface to serve as a support, etc.
    or to strengthen an angle formed by two surfaces' *O.E.D.*

Lock came off with it from the main Poſt. I found my Work was near finiſh'd, and that my Fate ſoon would be determined.

I was got to a Door opening in the lower Leads, which being only bolted on the Inſide, I open'd it with eaſe, and then clambred from the top of it to the higher Leads, and went over the Wall. I ſaw the Streets were lighted, the Shops being ſtill open, and therefore began to conſider what was neceſſary to be further done, as knowing that the ſmalleſt Accident would ſtill ſpoil the whole Workmanſhip, and was doubtful on which of the Houſes I ſhould alight. I found I muſt go back for the Blanket which had been my Covering a-nights in the Caſtle, which I accordingly did, and endeavoured to faſten my Stockings and that together, to leſſen my Deſcent, but wanted Neceſſaries ſo to do, and was therefore forc'd to make uſe of the Blanket alone. I fixt the ſame with the Chappel Spike into the Wall of *Newgate*, and dropt from it on the Turner's Leads, a Houſe adjoyning to the Priſon; 'twas then about Nine of the Clock, and the Shops not yet ſhut in. It fortunately happen'd, that the Garret Door on the Leads was open. I ſtole

ftole foftly down about two Pair of
Stairs, and then heard Company talking
in a Room; the Door open. My Irons
gave a fmall Clink, which made a Woman
cry, *Lord, what Noife is that?* A Man reply'd, *Perhaps the Dog or Cat*; and fo it
went off. I return'd up to the Garret, and
laid my felf down, being terribly fatigu'd;
and continu'd there for about two Hours,
and then crept down once more to the
Room where the Company were, and
heard a Gentleman taking his Leave, being very importunate to be gone, faying he
had difappointed Friends by not going
Home fooner. In about three Quarters
more the Gentleman took Leave, and
went, being lighted down Stairs by the
Maid, who, when fhe return'd, fhut the
Chamber-door; I then refolv'd at all Ha-
zards to follow, and flipt down Stairs,
but made a Stumble againft a Chamber-
door. I was inftantly in the Entry and
out at the Street Door, which I was fo
unmannerly as not to fhut after me. I
was once more, contrary to my own Ex-
pectation and that of all Mankind, a Freeman.

1 An EPISTLE from *Jack Sheppard* to the late L—d
G²—ll--r of *E---d*, who when *Sheppard* was ·ry'd, fent
2 for him to the *Chancery Bar*.

SINCE your Curiofity led you fo far
  As to fend for me once to the Chancery Bar
  To fhew what a Couple of Rafcals we were,
        Which no Body can deny.

Excufe me the Freedom in writing to thee,
For the World then allow'd they never did fee
A Pair fo well match'd as your Lordfhip and me,
        Which, &c.

At thy prefent Difgrace, my Lord never repine,
For Fame rings of Nothing, but thy Tricks, and mine,
And our Names will alike in all Hiftory fhine,
        Which, &c.

Tho' we two have made fo much Noife upon Earth,
Thy Fate would be now but a Subjeft of Mirth,
Sho'ud your Death be like mine, as we're equal in Birth,
        Which &c.

3 Were your Vertues, and mine to be weigh'd in a Scale,
I fear, honeft *Tom*, that thine would prevail,
For you broke through all Laws, while I only broke Jail,
        Which &c.

Yet Somenhing I hope to my Merit is due,
Since there ne'er was fo barefac'd a Bungler as you,
And that I'm the more dext'rous Rogue of the two,
        Which &c.

We who rob for our Living, if taken muft die;
Thofe who plunder poor Orphans, pray anfwer me why
4 They deferve not a Rope more than *Blueskin* and I?
        Which &c.

Tho' the Mafters were Rafcals, that you fhou'd fwing for't
Wou'd be damnable hard, for your Lordfhip in fhort
Was no more than the *Jonathan Wilde* of the Court.
        Which, &c.

Alike at the Helm you and *Jonathan* fit,
5 While your *Myrmidons* plunder, you feize what they get;
To fave their own Necks they muft lye at your Feet.
        Which, &c.

But *Jonathan's* Politicks muft be allow'd
Far better than thine; for he often has fhew'd
Himfelf he could fave, yet hang whom he wou'd.
        Which, &c.

But as thou, and thy Gang, muft come in for a Rope,
The Honour of being the Firft that's trafs'd up,
Is the principal Favour your Lordfhip can hope.
        Which no Body can deny.

Printed in the Year, 1725.

An Epistle from Jack Sheppard to the late L—d C—ll—r . .
1725. A Broadside. Complete text.

1. L—d C—ll—r of E—d: Lord Chancellor of England (head of the judiciary in England),
 Thomas Parker, 1st Earl of Macclesfield, 1666?-1732, impeached in 1725 for
 bribery, selling Masterships in Chancery, and other misdeeds, and found guilty.
2. *Chancery Bar*: the court of Chancery, the Lord Chancellor's court of equity; in
 reality Sheppard was tried at the King's Bench Court in Westminster Hall and
 it was as he was leaving the Hall that the Chancellor sent for him out of
 curiosity.
3. *Tom*: Thomas Parker
4. *Blueskin*: see headnote to *Harlequin Sheppard*
5. *Myrmidons*: subordinates who execute orders without protest or pity

68

III. The Political Background

There is no doubt about the political impact of *The Beggar's Opera* in its time, or about the political meanings of the play. Contemporary newspapers, journals, personal letters, and memoirs all demonstrate that Gay's piece was seen primarily as an attack on the incumbent Government, the Walpole Administration. Walpole's sins were well-known and very few of Gay's hits would have been missed by an audience trained to respond to such satire.

Gay was being both original and derivative. His dramatic creation of an entire symbolic world where everything and everyone has a price is brilliantly original. Lockit and Peachum are concerned only with the price of commodities, whether these be stolen goods, brides, or human lives. Newgate, not Westminster, is the capitol of this society, and Peachum's account book, not the Magna Carta, provides justice and law.

For his politica satire, however, Gay uses devices and comparisons familiar in Opposition writing, most tellingly the "great man" theme: the ironic praise of the scoundrel compared to the supposedly admirable character. In the *Opera* the great thief is equated with the great statesman: Jonathan Wild shadows forth Sir Robert Walpole. We must remember, though, that Gay avoids fixed associations. Just as Wild stands behind Peachum and Lockit and Macheath, so, at various times in the play, Peachum, Lockit, Macheath (whose mistresses suggest Sir Robert's well-known mistress, Molly Skerrett), and Bob Booty are all used to suggest Sir Robert.

Walpole in the 1720s did what he could, and it was much,

to eliminate a free press. Through spies, bribery, imprisonment, and the buying up of journalists and newspapers, he exercised a harsh control. The papers that managed to survive his repressive measures, such as *Mist's Weekly Journal*, had to proceed with caution. In two issues in June 1725, which we reprint, *Mist's* hit on the brilliant idea of writing about Walpole while apparently writing about Wild. Wild is a "statesman and a politician" who greatly admires the advice, "Get Money Son, honestly, if you can; but, however, get Money." Wild is a "great Man" no longer restrained by such old-fashioned values as "Honour and Conscience." Wild, the master thief, is the underworld equivalent of Walpole, the Chancellor of the Exchequer, who mysteriously grew enormously rich in office. Both are "great men," one commanding a gang, the other a party. The equation caught on in the public mind.

from *Mist's Weekly Journal*, 12 June 1725.

 S I was loitering the other Day in a Bookseller's Shop, I took up the next Thing to my Hand, in order to amuse my self, and it proved to be a Pamphlet newly published, containing the Life of that celebrated Statesman and Politician, the late Mr. *Jonathan Wild.*

I call him both Statesman and Politician, because I do not understand them to be synonimous Terms; for, I conceive, it is well known to many Persons, still living, that there have been some Statesmen in the World who never were so much as suspected of being Politicians, as well as an infinite Number of Politicians who never were Statesmen. —— But the extraordinary Person, of whom we are Writing, was an Instance of both.

The Historian has curiously enough accounted by what sort of Arts *Jonathan* made himself considerable, and drew the Eyes of the admiring World upon him, he has given many Instances [1] of his deep Fetch in Politicks, when he describes that Form, or rather that System of Government which he established over the Thieves.

I shall not touch upon any Thing taken Notice of by that Writer, but as he has shewn him in [2] his publick Capacity, I shall describe him in his Closet, and give the Observations I made by a personal Acquaintance, and long Conversation with this great Genius.

Perhaps the Readers may smile to hear me speak in such high Terms, of one who (to call Things by their proper Names) was no better than a *Thief.* —— I own that the Word *Thief* is generally apply'd by People, who do not value themselves upon their Politeness, to Persons of Mr. *Wild's* Character. —— Yet I suppose it will be granted, that a Person may be a Rogue, and yet be a great Man, which may excuse me for employing more gentle Terms when I only speak of him as a Man of Parts.

Mr. WILD (like other great Men) had a Turn of Thought peculiar to himself; he was not for following the common Road, he was for going out of the beaten Paths in Search of Adventures, nor was he less singular in his Notions ; it was his Opinion, that Men of Parts (in which Class he sometimes included —— Thieves and idle Fellows) should be maintained by the Publick, and whether it was done by picking their Pockets, or boldly by taking their Money by Force, he thought it much the same Thing. —— He was a great Admirer of that Advice, which, it is said, a Man when he was dying gave his Son, —— *Get Money Son, honestly, if you can ; but, however, get Money* ; and would often say, it must be a wise Man, who pronounced that Sentence.

Tho' he was a Man much given to Contemplation, yet he had read Men more than Books, for he was of Opinion, there was more to be learned thereby, since we are to live by the Living, not by the Dead ; however, he had con-

versed enough with Books to pass for a Man of some Erudition. — I have often seen his Library, which consisted of Books, few in Number, but well chosen ; I will say nothing of Tradesmen's Shop-Books, which he only dealt in his Way of Business, or, I may say, as he could lay his Hands upon them, for they yielded Money.

But the Authors which he study'd most were *Ma-* [3] *chiavel, The English Rogue, The Lives of the High-* [4,5] *Way Men, Cook upon Littleton, Echard's History of* [6,7] *England, a Collection of Sessions Papers,* and *Corne-* [8] *lius Tacitus.* [9]

Thus his Library consisted of a mixture of Politicks, Law and History. By what he had studied of *English* History, he found out that there are more wise Men to be met with in these Times, than any former Age could boast of; for heretofore it appeared to him as if Men were apt to give in to some foolish Prejudices which hinder a Man's thriving and growing great in the World, such as Honour and Conscience, which now, says he, your busy pushing People look upon to be Chimeras, and therefore you see that —— and —— and many more, who are rising People, don't make the least Pretence to either.

It is certain he understood no Latin, for he had employ'd his Time to greater Advantage than in learning Words; but as he had observed some Latin Sentences now and then scattered thro' my Works, an Affectation, we, the present Set of Writers are much addicted to, he took me to be something of a Scholar, and therefore consulted me in explaining to him the Annals of *Tacitus* : When I read to him how slavishly the *Romans* submitted themselves to be then governed, he shook his Head, and said, those were fine Times to get Money ; for when the Senate and all the Magistrates judged and decreed no otherwise than as they were directed by the Emperor, or his Favorites, an enterprizing Man (under which Denomination he included all

---

3. *Machiavel*: Machiavelli, who in *The Prince* offers reputedly amoral advice to rulers

4. *The English Rogue*: by Richard Head and Francis Kirkman, 1665-74

5. *The Lives of the High-Way Men*: Captain Alexander Smith, *A Complete History of the Lives and Robberies of the most notorious Highwaymen* . . . 1714; 1719.

6. *Cook upon Littleton*: Coke upon Lyttleton, famous legal text

7. *Echard's History of England*: Laurence Echard's *History of England*, 1707-18.

8. *a Collection of Sessions Papers*: accounts of criminal trials

9. *Cornelius Tacitus*: the Roman historian, ca.55-120.

---

1. Fetch: contrivance, stratagem
2. in his Closet: in private

Rogues) had an easy Game to play, for, says he, it was but touching the Courtiers (I speak in his own Terms) and all was rug; *for Courtiers are always obsequious to the Touch.*

As he often frequented the Plays, partly for Pleasure, and partly for Profit (having generally Hands at Work there) he much admired that Scene in the *Recruiting Officer,* where the Constable bringing a Man before a Magistrate. —— The Magistrate demands of the Constable what he has to say against that Man, *nothing,* (answers the Constable,) *but that he's an honest Man.* —— This Sentence always tickled *Jonathan,* and he said, he had rather to have been Author of that Sentence than the whole play besides, for, added he, this is Natural, this is taken from Life.

He bore a very great Veneration for Men of Parts, and has often been heard to say, that Men of Wit, who have no other Inheritance to maintain them, should ride the World, and bridle and saddle the rest of Mankind one way or other ; but he abhorr'd Quacks or Pretenders in any Art or Science, and therefore he commended the Policy of the Jesuites, who having the Education of Youth committed to them, took Care that no Fool should be admitted into their Society, and he thought, that the *Rogues* in *Great Britain* should imitate the same Policy ; for tho' the Faculty, as he sometimes merrily stiled it, was in a very prosperous Way, yet so many Fools and Bunglers were daily thrusting themselves into it, that with a

heavy Heart he foresaw they would *bring Roguery into Discredit, at last, with the World.*—— This was owing, he said, to Mens mistaking their Inclination for Genius, There are, no doubt on't, at this Time, added he, great Numbers of People possess'd with strong Inclinations for entring into our Society, as they shew by their daily Actions, and they want *Parts,* they have the Will without the Skill, Address or Policy, which are the Qualities that must bear up Persons of our Profession in the World.——Where's the *Merit* of cheating *Women or Children, Lunaticks, or Ideots ?* who are not in any Capacity of defending themselves.—— I would expel such a mean spirited Professor from my Society, as a Person *unworthy of the Name of Rogue* and unfit for any ingenious Enterprize ; I should contemn him as I would that bragging Soldier, who boasting of his Courage, said, that he had cut off the Leg of an Enemy in the last Battle : It had been braver, methinks, says one, who stood by, to have cut off his Head : Oh ! says he, that was cut off before.

N. B. The excellent Letter, sign'd J. Smith is come to Hand, and if we could give it the Distinction we think it deserves it should be to print it in Letters of Gold, but as there *, a certain Person in the World, at present, little too strong for us, we hope our Corre* ndent will take that for an Excuse.

from *Mist's Weekly Journal*, 19 June 1725

I N my laſt I began to enter upon the Character of the late celebrated Mr. *Jonathan Wild*, of moſt ingenious and moſt roguiſh *Memory* ; — but, I find now, that I only drew the Out-lines of his Figure, and that much remains ſtill undone towards giving the World a right Idea, not only of the Capacity of this extraordinary Man, but of that Plan which he had form'd to himſelf for the Conduct and Government of Life.

Therefore I think fit to obſerve, that as his known Intimacy with ſome Perſons of conſiderable Ra... ¹ ... Occaſion to ſuſpect that he was, at Bottom, the Projector, at leaſt Adviſer of ſeveral very ſtrange Things, which, of late Years have appeared in the World (to his no ſmall Diſcredit.) —— As I would give the *Devil* his *Due*, ſo I ſhall endeavour to clear him from thoſe falſe Aſperſions which ſeem to blacken his Memory, being willing to ſet the World right in that Affair.

Among other Things, he intirely diſclaim'd his ² having any Hand in the late *South-Sea* Scheme, and proteſted he had no Acquaintance with Mr. ³ *Robert Knight* ; nor would he own that he was any way concern'd in the Bubble call'd the *Bahama Iſlands*, nor in the *Welſh Copper*, nor in the *Braſs*, or *Iron*, or *Deal Boards*, or any of thoſe ridiculous Projects which in thoſe Times ſtarted up every ⁴ Day in *'Change-Alley*, and died in a *Week* —— Not that it would have diſturb'd his Conſcience to have got Money that Way (which he frankly own'd to me;) but his Pride was ſuch, that he ſcorn'd to be concern'd in any *Roguery* where there was not ſome Wit and Ingenuity in the Contrivance, and ſome Danger in the Execution ; therefore he uſed to ſpeak with the utmoſt Conʈempt ⁵ of a Sort of Men known by the Name of *Penſioners* ; an Office, he ſaid, no Man of the leaſt Spirit or Parts would accept, becauſe the Buſineſs may be done by *Ideots*, as well as Men of Senſe, and he was for putting them upon a *Foot* with Scavengers : and he often proteſted he never made uſe of any (though the World ſuſpected he did,) ſwearing he never would give them Bread, for he would have no *Fools* in his Commonwealth.

The Succeſs of all his Enterprizes was owing to that State-Maxim of taking *Times and Opportunities*, which he ſtrictly obſerv'd ; and which, he ſaid, was the Life and Soul of Buſineſs, as might be ſeen by what was done in his Expedition to the Inſtalment at *Windſor*, where he ſucceeded, in ⁶ laying hold of Things he never could have come at, if that Opportunity had been ſlipp'd.

He communicated to me a Deſign he had of ⁷ getting a Treatiſe wrote *de Legibus Naturæ* ; under which Title, Theft, and all Kinds of Knavery ſhould be recommended as vertuous and honourable Actions ; and that they were juſtifiable by the Laws of Nature, which teach us to ſeek our own Good ; and that he intended to employ the ⁸ ingenious Pen of the Author of the *Fable of the Bees* for that Purpoſe, whom he look'd upon to be equal to the Subject ; and he confeſs'd to me, that it was he who gave that Author the Hint of a Thing which makes ſo conſiderable a Figure in his Book, viz. that where he endeavours to prove robbing on the Highway to be *for the Good of the Publick.*

When his Troubles came upon him, I viſited him, in order to found what his Sentiments were of his own Condition. ——For, as it was reported, that there would be a numerous Train of Indictments brought againſt him, ſome of which were for Crimes long ſince committed, I was willing to know of him, whether he intended to ⁹ plead the Act of Grace ? To which he anſwer'd in the *Negative*, adding, that he ſcorn'd it ; —— for, ſays he, an Act of Grace is to *ſome People* like a Harbour to Pyrates, where they lay up in Safety what they have pillaged upon the open Seas ; whereas a Man of true Spirit would rather keep ¹⁰ the Seas, and truſt his own Courage and Reſolution than to have Recourſe to ſuch Shifts as plainly diſcover both his Guilt and his Fear.—— Many ſuch wiſe Sayings often dropp'd from him, which I have laid up in the Table of my Memory, deſigning, ſome Time or other, to publiſh them for the univerſal Good of Mankind.

Though the Application of this Simile was juſt and well hit, yet I ſuſpected there was a little Vanity in the Declaration ; and that, as the Fox, ¹¹

1. Illegible; should read: able Rank gave Men Occasion to suspect that he was, at Bottom, the Projector, at least Adviser
2. *South-Sea* Scheme: the great financial disaster in 1720 caused by the vastly inflated prices of South Sea Company Stock
3. Mr. *Robert Knight*: the South Sea Company's cashier
4. *Change-Alley*: 'Wall Street'
5. *Pensioners*: those who receive pensions or payment from the government, usually with the understanding that they will vote for government measures
6. the Instalment at Windsor: an Instalment of Knights of the Garter at Windsor, where Wild was supervising robberies
7. de Legibus Naturae: on the laws of Nature
8. the author of the *Fable*: *The Fable of the Bees: or, Private Vices, Publick Benefits* (1714), written by Bernard Mandeville, 1670-1733.
9. Act of Grace: a free and general pardon, granted by Act of Parliament
10. Illegible; should read: the Seas and trust his own Courage and Resolution than to have Recourse to such Shifts as
11. the Fox: in Aesop's fable of the fox and the grapes

who could not come at the Grapes which his Chaps water'd at, said, at going off, they were sowre; so *Jonathan* slighted the Act of Grace, from a Consciousness that he could not be protected by it; therefore I put the Question to him directly, whether he thought his Crimes could, by any Construction, come under the Cover of the said Act? ————He made me no direct Answer, but smil'd, and said, *The Act was not of his drawing up.*

But since I have taken Notice of his Erudition, and hinted at his wise Sayings, I think it will not be amiss to inform the World, that for some Years past, at his leisure Hours, he employed himself constantly in writing the *History of his own Times,* which History he was pleas'd to put into my Hands, having first exacted a Promise from me not to publish it till seven *Years after his Death,* which Request, as I intend religiously to observe, I hope my courteous Correspondents, to whom I am sometimes obliged, and whose Curiosity (no doubt) will be rais'd up to a Pitch of Impatience, will not expect or desire that I should inviolate the said Promise by publishing any Part of these

Memoirs in my weekly Labours, till the said Time is expired.

I shall only observe in general, that the said History is very curious in its Kind, a great many State Intrigues being there laid open and accounted for, and the secret Causes which produced them discover'd, that it is, as to Stile and Truth, Matter much preferrable to another History of the same Kind lately publish'd, and is free both from the Vanity and Rancour which makes up the greatest Part of that History,

But now that I've said so much of this extraordinary Man, methinks his Character must still appear imperfect, unless I give some Account of his Principles both as to Church and State, there being no *Englishman* altogether indifferent upon those Articles.————As to Religion he was a Freethinker, and I'm afraid, a little inclin'd *to Atheism,* (if I may be allow'd to call that a Religion,) As to Party, he was both in Principle and Practice a right Modern Whig, according to the Definition of those Gentlemen, which is expres'd in this their Motto,————*Keep what you got, and get what you can.*

12. Illegible; should read: himself constantly in writing the *History of his own*

13. *History of his own Times*: a parody of the *History of my own Times* (1st vol., 1723), by Gilbert Burnet, a celebrated Whig bishop

The most important Opposition paper, the one most hated by Walpole, was *The Craftsman*, which first appeared on 5 December 1726. It was founded by Bolingbroke, who had gathered around him at his farm at Dawley a distinguished literary circle opposed to Walpole that included Gay and Pope.

Bolingbroke's "The Vision of Camilick" is an impressive and characteristically indirect attack on Walpole. In it Camilick, a Persian prophet, dreams of a king and his nobles all adoring a holy constitution, and finally living in peace. This utopia is upset by a man with a bag of gold who manages to turn all from the holy parchment to a worship of gold. For the twentieth-century reader "The Vision of Camilick" is a good example of the kind of journalistic attack made upon Walpole before Pope and Gay published theirs. What Bolingbroke is saying about England and Walpolian materialism in the rather clumsy form of Oriental vision is very close to what Gay is saying wittily and dramatically.

FRIDAY, *January* 27.

 AVING as yet given the Reader little befides grave difcourfes on publick matters, and forefeeing that, during the Seffion of Parliament, I fhall be obliged to continue daily in the fame track, I am willing to take this one opportunity of prefenting him with fomething which has no relation at all to Publick affairs, but is of a nature purely amufing, and entirely void of Reflection upon any perfon whatfoever.   My

1. motto In Hoc Signo vinces: In this sign thou shalt conquer

My Friend *Alvarez* (a man not unknown to many here, by his frequent journeys to *England*) did fome time fince make me a prefent of a *Perfian* manufcript, which he met with while he follow'd the fortunes of *Miriweis.* An exact tranflation of the firft Chapter has been made at my requeft by the learned Mr. *Solomon Negri*, and is as follows;

The firft Vifion of Camilick.

IN the Name of God, ever merciful, and of *Haly* his prophet. I flept in the plains of *Bagdad*, and I dreamed a Dream. I lifted my eyes, and I faw a vaft Field, pitch'd with the Tents of the mighty, and the Strong ones of the Earth in array of Battle. I obferv'd the arms and enfigns of either hoft: in the banners of the one were pictur'd a Crown and Sceptre, and upon the fhields of the Soldiers were engraven fcourges, chains, iron maces, axes, and all kinds of inftruments of Violence. The ftandards of the other bore the Crown and Sceptre alfo; but the devices on the fhields were the Balance, the olive wreath, the plough-fhare, and other emblematical figures of juftice, peace, law, and liberty. Between thefe two armies, I faw a King come forth, and fign a large *Roll of parchment*, at which loud fhouts of acclamation were heard

heard from every Quarter. The *Roll* it-
felf flew up into the air, and appear'd
over their heads, encompaffed with Rays
of glory. I obferved that where-ever the
fecond Army moved, this glorious Apparition attended them, or rather the army
feemed only to move, as that guided or
directed. Soon after, I faw both thefe
hofts engaged, and the whole face of the
land overfpread with Blood. I faw the
King, who had fign'd and broken that *Sacred Charter*, drink out of a golden cup,
fall into convulfions, gafp and die.

I then faw another King take his
place, who, in the moft folemn manner,
engaged to make the Words contain'd
in the *Roll* the Guide of his Actions;
but notwithftanding this, I faw both
Armies again encounter. I faw the King
a Prifoner; I faw his Son relieve him,
and I faw the Chiefs of the other army put to death. Yet that victorious
Son himfelf bow'd his Head to the *Parchment*, which now appear'd with fuller
luftre than before. S veral other battles
enfued, with vaft flaughter on both fides,
during which the *Celeftial Volume* was
fometimes clouded over; but ftill again
exerted its rays, and after every cloud
appear'd the brighter. I obferved thofe
Heroes, who fought beneath it, tho' e-
ver fo unfortunate, not once to abate
their

their courage, while they had the leaft
glimpfe of that heavenly apparition in
their view; and even Thofe whom I
faw overthrown, pierced with ghaftly
wounds, and panting in death, refign'd
their lives in fmiles, and with eyes caft
up to that glorious object. At laft the
long contention ceafed: I beheld both Armies unite and move together under the
fame divine influence. I faw one King
twelve times bow down before the bright
Phænomenon, which from thence forward
fpread a light over the whole land, and
defcending nearer to the Earth, the beams
of it grew fo warm as it approach'd, that
the hearts of the inhabitants leap'd for
joy. The face of war was no more. The
fame Fields, which had fo long been the
fcene of death and defolation, were now
cover'd with golden harvefts. The Hills
were cloath'd with fheep; the Woods
fung with gladnefs; Plenty laugh'd in the
Valleys; Induftry, Commerce, and Liberty danced hand in hand thro' the
Cities.

While I was delighting myfelf with
this amiable Profpect, the fcene entirely
changed; the fields and armies vanifhed,
and I faw a large and magnificent Hall,
refembling the Great *Divan* or Council of
the Nation; at the upper end of it,
under a canopy, I beheld the *Sacred*

S   *Cove-*

Covenant, fhining as the Sun. The Nobles of the land were there affembled;
they proftrated themfelves before it,
and they fung an Hymn. *Let the heart*
of the King be glad; for his people are hap-
py! may the light of the Covenant be a
2 *lanthorn to the feet of the Judges; for by*
this fhall they feparate Truth from falfhood.
O Innocence rejoice! for by this light fhalt
thou walk in Safety, nor fhall the oppreffor
take hold on thee. O Juftice be exceeding
Glad! for by this light all thy Judgments
fhall be decreed with wifdom, nor fhall any
Man fay thou haft erred. Let the hearts of
all the people be glad! for this have their
Grandfathers died, in this have their Fa-
thers rejoiced, and in this may their Po-
fterity rejoice evermore!

Then all the Rulers took a Solemn
Oath to preferve it inviolate and un-
changed, and to facrifice their lives and
their fortunes, rather than fuffer themfelves
or their children to be deprived of fo inva-
luable a Bleffing.

After this I faw another and larger affembly come forward into the Hall, and
join the firft. Thefe paid the fame adora-
tions to the *Covenant,* took the fame oath,
they fung the fame Hymn, and added a
folemn Form of Imprecation to this effect.
Let the words of the Roll *be for ever in*
our eyes, and graven on our hearts; and
                                            accurfed

---

2. lanthorn: lantern

accurfed be he who layeth hands on the
fame; accurfed be He who fhall remove
this writing from the people, or who fhall
hide the law thereof from the King. Let
that man be cut off from the earth; let
his Riches be fcatter'd as the Duft; let
his wife be the wife of the people; let not
his firft-born be rank'd among the nobles;
let his palaces be deftroy'd; let his gardens
be as a defart, having no water; let his 3
horfes and his horfemen be overthrown;
and let his dogs devour their carcaffes!
—In the midft of thefe execrations enter'd
a man, drefs'd in a plain habit, with
a purfe of gold in his hand. He threw
himfelf forward into the room, in a
bluff ruffianly manner. A Smile, or rather a Snear, fat on his countenance. His
Face was brouz'd over with a glare of 4
Confidence. An arch malignity leer'd in
his eye. Nothing was fo extraordinary
as the effect of this perfon's appearance.
They no fooner faw him, but they all
turn'd their faces from the Canopy, and
fell proftrate before him. He trod over
their backs, without any ceremony, and
march'd directly up to the Throne. He
open'd his Purfe of Gold, which he took
out in Handfuls, and fcattered amongft
the Affembly. While the greater Part
were engaged in fcrambling for thefe Pieces,
He feiz'd, to my inexpreffible furprife,

S 2   with-

---

3. *desart*: desert
4. brouz'd: brushed, painted

without the leaſt Fear, upon the ſacred
Parchment it ſelf. He rumpled it rudely
up, and cramm'd it into his pocket. Some
of the people began to murmur. He threw
more Gold, and they were pacified. No
ſooner was the *Parchment* taken away, but
in an inſtant I ſaw half the auguſt Aſſem-
bly in Chains; nothing was heard thro'
the whole Divan, but the noiſe of Fetters,
and clank of Irons. I ſaw Pontiffs in their
eccleſiaſtical habits, and Senators, clad in
ermine, linked together like the moſt ig-
nominious ſlaves. Terror and amazement
were impreſſed on every countenance,
except that of ſome few, to whom the
Man continued diſperſing his gold. This
He did, till his purſe became empty; then
He dropt it; but then too, in the very
ſame moment, He himſelf dropt with it to
the ground; that and the date of his power at once expired; He ſunk, and ſunk for
ever. The radiant *volume* again aroſe, a-
gain ſhone out, and reaſſumed its place
above the throne; the throne, which had
been darkened all this time, was now fil-
led with the effulgence of the glory, which
darted from it. Every chain dropped off
in an inſtant; every face regained its former chearfulneſs; Heaven and Earth re-
ſounded with *Liberty! Liberty!* and the
HEART OF THE KING WAS
GLAD WITHIN HIM.

Shortly after the first performance of the *Opera*, spies for *The Senator*, an administration paper financed by Walpole, who were planted in the staff of *The Craftsman*, learned what political hay the Opposition paper intended to reap from the *Opera*. Accordingly, 'Elkanah Pikestaff' predicts to 'Abraham Standfast' in *The Senator* on 16 February what *The Craftsman* will print the next day. As predicted, a long article appeared, written by one 'Phil. Harmonicus' to the fictional editor, Caleb D'Anvers, underlining and emphasizing the political interpretations of the *Opera*. The article was later reprinted with the title *A Key To The Beggar's Opera*.

from *The Senator*, 16 February 1728.

I have been well acquaintd with many of his [Caleb D'Anvers] Predecessors, who have, like him, made very noisy Entrances on the Stage, but soon pass'd off, and are now sleeping in profound Obscurity with their Ancestors. I flatter myself, that from the first Appearance of such a Writer I can see to his utmost Extent; and am able to fathom his depth, and judge critically of the Danger we are to expect from him. You wou'd be surprized perhaps, if I shou'd be sanguine enough to prophesy of the sort of Entertainment which he will exhibit To-morrow; No one will imagine that I have a secret Intelligence with him; and yet I am vain enough of my Skill in Prediction to advertise the Publick, that he will To-morrow be in high Spirits upon the late Election in the City, and like the Fly in the Fable will not fail to take the Credit of it to himself. I cou'd even venture to go further, and to assure the Publick that as he has frequently borrow'd his Wit from the Playhouse, and made *Harlequin* stand for a much greater Character, so he will very soon make use of the same Expedient. He will find out a farther Meaning than every Body sees in The Beggars Opera. Mac-heath, he will tell us, is so often mentioned as a very great Man,[1] is introduc'd with so many great Circumstances, so full of Vices, so entangled with Perplexities and Distresses, that he cou'd never be drawn for the sake of representing a Highwayman.—Time will show whether I am deceiv'd in my Art; but at present I take this to be a Bait which a small Genius like his cannot avoid nibbling at. If I succeed, you shall hear again from
   Dear Mr. Standfast
   Your most humble Servant
   Elkanah Pikestaff

A Key To The Beggar's Opera In A Letter To Caleb Danvers, Esq; in Christopher Bullock, Woman's Revenge; Or, A Match in Newgate . . . The Second Edition . . . London: Printed for J. Roberts in Warwick-Lane. 1728. Pp. [69]-76. The complete text of the key.

---

1. I.xi; III.xv.

A

KEY

TO THE

BEGGAR'S OPERA.

IN A

LETTER

TO

Caleb Danvers, Efq;

Totus *mundus agit* Hiſtrionem ;
Anglicè,
The Stage turns all the World to Ridicule.

S I R,

I Sent you, ſome Months ago, an Account
of the declining State of the *Royal, Bri-* 1
tiſh Academy, occaſioned by the Diſputes
between the two famous *Rival Queens* and
their *contending Factions,* whether the *firſt Part*
in the *Opera* belonged to *Cuzzoni* or *Fauſtina* ; 2
which

---

1. *Royal, British Academy*: which sponsored the Italian opera
2. *Cuzzoni* or *Faustina*: Francesca Cuzzoni and Faustina Bordoni, the two leading
   prima donnas; see introduction to 'Opera and Music'

which have been since carried to such an
Height, that (like most other Animosities)
they have almost brought that *mighty State* itself into Contempt.   We have seen it dwin-
dle by Degrees, for a Year or two past, till it
is, at *length*, in a Manner, *deserted*, even by
3   its greatest, quondam *Admirers, Subscribers* and
4   *Directors*——*O! Tempora! O! Mores!* that e-
5   ver the Theatre in the *Hay-Market* shou'd be
6   obliged to yield to that in *Lincolns-Inn-Fields!*
——that the coarse Ribaldry and vulgar Catches
of a *Newgate Hero* shou'd prevail over the me-
7   lodious Enchantments of *Senesino!* whilst the
once celebrated *Cuzzoni* and *Faustina* lay aside
their former Emulation, and, with united Resentment, behold the Palm of *Precedence* given
to pretty Miss *Polly Peachum*——with a P
8   I hope the *Beaumonde* will give me Leave to
observe (which nothing but the present *melancholy occasion* could extort from me) that this is
an undeniable Mark of a *vitiated Taste* and a
degenerate, licentious Age, which delights in
seeing Things of the greatest Importance turned to *Ridicule*.   Who can help being surprized
to find two of his Majesty's *Theatres* prostitut-
ed in this Manner; and made the popular En-
gines for conveying not only *Scandal* and *Scur-
rility*, but even *Sedition* and *Treason* through
the Kingdom? Have we not, lately, seen the
awful Solemnity of a *Coronation* openly bur-
lesqued at both Theatres? Have not the *Nobles*, the *Prelates*, the *Judges* and *Magistrates* of
9   the Land been personated by *Miller, Johnson*
and *Harper* at one House; and by *Harlequin*
and his Associates at the other? Have not *some
Persons*, in a *certain, honourable Assembly*, been
tra-

---

3. quondam: former
4. *O! Tempora! O! Mores!:* O the times, the customs!
5. *Hay-Market*: where the Italian opera was performed
6. *Lincolns-Inn-Fields*: the Theatre Royal, Lincoln's Inn Fields, where *The Beggar's Opera* was first performed
7. *Senesino*: Francesco Bernardi Senesino, c.1680-c.1750, one of the most famous
of 18th century castrati; he sang frequently in Handel's operas
8. *Beaumonde*: fashionable society

traduced, for almoſt *thirty Nights* together, in
the Character of a *wrong-headed Country Knight,* 10
of *mean Intellects* and a *broken Fortune* ? And,
laſtly, is not the *Opera-State* itſelf become the
Subject of Mirth and Deriſion to *crouded* and
clapping Audiences.

  Though I am a *conſtant Spectator* of the *Beggar's Opera,* which affords me a *nightly Entertainment,* and have always had a great Reſpect
for Mr. *R—ch* ; yet I am often ſurprized at 11
the late *unprecedented Inſolence* and *Audaciouſ-
neſs of that Gentleman* ; *and have often wonder-
ed that ſuch Entertainments are ſuffered to be
exhibited, Night after Night, to the whole Town,
with* Impunity.— *How could it enter into his
Head to turn the fine Songs of the* Opera *into
ſuch high Ridicule ? He knows very well* WHO
goes to, *and takes Delight in* thoſe Diverſions.
It was impoſſible to think that all the Diſap-
pointments *in the World could have tranſport-
ed Him to this Degree. But as the beſt Actions
are liable to malicious and invidious Turns, this
innocent Amuſement of the——* muſt *not eſcape* 12
the Ridicule of righteous Mr. R—ch. ———*Did
He mean to inſinuate by this, that nothing but*
Sing-ſong, empty Sound *and* Geſticulation
pleaſe and recommend at an Opera? *Or did He
hope, that* other, harſh Inferences *would be
made by the* Diſaffected, *which I deteſt, and He*
dares *not name ?*

  It will, I know be ſaid, by theſe *libertine
Stage-Players,* that the *Satire* is *general* ; and
that it diſcovers a *Conſciouſneſs* of Guilt for
any *particular Man* to apply it to *Himſelf.*
But they ſeem to forget that there are ſuch
Things as *Innuendo's,* (a never-failing Method.
of

---

9. *Miller, Johnson* and *Harper:* Joseph Miller, Benjamin Johnson, John Harper,
   actors at Drury Lane theatre. In November 1727 coronation scenes were played
   in *Jane Shore, Virtue Betray'd; or, Anna Bullen,* and *Henry VIII,* but the above
   actor's names do not appear in the casts. 'The other' house, Lincoln's Inn
   Fields, played a burlesque coronation as an afterprice, 24 November 1727.
10. *Country Knight:* Macheath
11. Mr. R—ch: John Rich, manager of the Theatre Royal, Lincoln's Inn Fields where
   The Beggar's Opera was first performed
12. the —: the rich, who patronised the Italian opera

of explaining *Libels*) and that, when all the
Town fees through their Defign, it is unreafon-
able to fuppofe *thofe Perfons only* incapable
of underftanding it, to whom it belongs to
punifh fuch Enormities. Nay the very *Title*
of this Piece and the *principal Character*, which
is that of an *Highwayman*, fufficiently difcover the mifchievous Defign of it; fince by
this Character every Body will underftand
13 *One*, who makes it his Bufinefs arbitrarily to
levy and *collect* Money on the People for his
own Ufe, and of which he always dreads to give
14 *any Account*——Is not this *fquinting* with a
Vengeance, and wounding *Perfons in Authority*
through the Sides of a *common Malefactor* ?

But I fhall go ftill deeper into this Affair
and undertake to prove, beyond all Difpute,
that the *Beggar's Opera* is the moft venemous
15 *allegorical Libel* againft the G————t that
hath appeared for many Years paft.

There are fome Perfons, who efteem *Lockit*,
the *Keeper*, or *prime Minifter* of *Newgate*, to be
the *Hero* of the Piece; to juftify which O-
pinion, they take Notice that He is fet forth,
16 on the Stage, in the Perfon of Mr. *Hall*, as
a very *corpulent, bulky* Man; and that he hath
a *Brother*, named *Peachum*, who, as reprefented by Mr. *Hippfely*, appears to be a *little, awk-
ward flovenly* Fellow. They obferve farther
17 that thefe *two Brothers* have a numerous Gang
of *Thieves* and *Pick-pockets* under their Direction, with whom they divide the *Plunder*,
18,19 and whom they either *fcreen* or *tuck up*, as
their *own Intereft* and the *prefent Occafion* requires——But I am obliged to reject this Interpretation as erroneous, however plaufible
it

---

13. *One*: Sir Robert Walpole
14. *squinting*: alluding
15. *G_t*: Government
16. Mr. *Hall*, Mr. *Hippsely*: Hall and Hippisley, actors at Lincoln's Inn Fields, the
    original Lockit and Peachum
17. two *Brothers:* probably a glance at Robert Walpole and his brother Horatio or
    his brother-in-law Townshend, who for a time shared power with him.
18. *screen*: protect (Walpole had been accused for years of screening guilty directors
    of the South Sea Company against punishment for misuse of funds)
19. *tuck up*: hang

It may be, and to embrace another, which is more generally received; *viz.* that Captain *Macbeath*, who hath alfo a goodly *Prefence*, and hath a tolerable *Bronze* upon his Face, is de- 20 figned for the *principal Charader.* and drawn to afperfe *fomebody in Authority.* He is repre- 21 fented at the Head of a Gang of *Robbers*, who promife to ftand by Him againft all the *En-quiries* and *coercive Force* of the *Law*, He is often call'd a *Great Man,*——particularly 22 in the two following Paffages, *viz. It grieves one's Heart to take off a great* Man.—*what a moving Thing it is, to fee a* Great Man *in Di-ftrefs*; which by the Bye, feems to be an *Innuendo* that fome *Great Man* will fpeedily fall into *Diftrefs.* Soon after his *firft Appearance* 23 on the Stage, He is *taken up* and *confin'd* for a certain, *flippery Prank* on the Road; but hath the good Fortune to *efcape* that Time, by the Help of a trufty *Friend.* He is afterwards retaken in much *better Plight* and *Apparel* than before, and ordered for *Execution;* which is prevented, for no other Reafon that I can fee, than that the *Poet* is afraid of offending the *Criticks*, by making an *Opera* end with a *tragical Cataftrophe*; for he plainly tells us, that this Obfervance of *dramatick Rules*, in one Point, hath made Him violate *poetical Juftice* in another, and fpoil a very good *Moral*; *viz. That the* lower People have their *Vices in a Degree as well as the* Rich, *and are* punifhed *for them,* ——— innuendo, that *rich* 24 People *never are.*

But herein, I confefs, the *Author* feems to be fomewhat *inconfiftent*, by ranking his Hero *Macbeath*, whom He had before called a *Great Man*, amongft the *lower People.* But this, per-

G haps

---

20. *Bronze*: brazenness (Walpole had a florid complexion and great equanimity in the face of charges of ill-doing)
21. *somebody in Authority*: Sir Robert Walpole
22. *a great Man*: I.xi.
23. *Distress*: III.xv.
24. punished *for them*: III.xvi.

haps, might be done for a *Blind*; and then, no doubt, the *Reprieve* was brought in, to inculcate the same *Moral*, in a stronger Manner; *viz.* by an *Example* of a *Great Man*, and a *notorious Offender*, who escapes with *Impunity*.

His *satirical* strokes upon *Ministers*, *Courtiers* and *Great Men*, in general, abound in every Part of this most *insolent Performance*. In one place, where *Polly Peachum* acknowledges her Match with *Captain Macheath*, her Father breaks out in a Passion, with these Words, *What, marry an* Highwayman! *why, he'll*
25   *make as bad an Husband as a Lord*——*innuendo*, that all *Lords* make *bad Husbands*.————Soon after, when *Miss Polly* questions her Spouse's *Constancy*, he tells her *that you might sooner tear a* Pension *out of the Hands of a* Courtier,
26   *than tear Him from Her*———*innuendo*, that all *Courtiers* have *Pensions*. In the following Song, the Employment of a *Statesman* is, by *innuendo*, made as bad or worse than that of *Jonathan Wild*, represented under the Character of *Peachum*; which he introduces by a general *Libel* on Men of all Professions, even the most *sacred*, in order to make that of a *Statesman* more black and vile.

> *Through all the Employments of Life,*
>   *Each Neighbour abuses his Brother,*
> *Whore and* Rogue *they call* Husband *and*
>   *All Profession be-rogue one another. (* Wife,
> *The* Priest *calls the* Lawyer *a Cheat,*
>   *The* Lawyer *be-knaves the* Divine;
> *And the* Statesman, *because He's so great,*
27   *Thinks his* Trade *as honest as* mine.

The *second Act* begins with a Scene of *Highway-men*, drinking together, who solemnly promise

_____

25. *as a Lord*: I.viii.
26. *Him from Her*: I.xiii.
27. *as* mine: Air I.

promise never to *betray* one another for *Interest*
or any *other Motive*; upon which one of them
gets up and says; *Shew me a Gang of* Courtiers,
who can say as much— *innuendo*, that *Courtiers* 28
have less Honesty than Highway-men. — In another Place, It is said *that* our Gang *can't trust
one another any more than other People*— *innu-* 29
endo———

　In a Scene between *Peachum* and his *Brother
Lockit, Peachum* takes upon Him to say *that He
does not like these* long Arrears *of the G——t* 30
(innuendo, that the G——t *is in Arrear)* — A-
gain, says he, *can it be expected that we should
hang our Acquaintance for nothing, when* our
Betters *will hardly* save *theirs without being paid
for it.——Innuendo,* that *some Persons* have been 31
well paid for *saving,* or *screening* their *former
Acquaintance.* — He says farther *that unless the
People in Employment* pay better *(innuendo* that
they pay *very badly) He shall let* other Rogues
live besides Theirs—*innuendo* that there are o- 32
ther Rogues.—

　He goes on with observing *that, in one Re-
spect, their* Employment *may be reckoned* disho-
nest, *because, like* Great Statesmen, *they encourage* those, *who betray their* Friends; — which 33
contains, by *Innuendo,* a Confirmation of that
ridiculous as well as scandalous vulgar Error,
that *great Statesmen frequently betray their Friends.*
　Upon this, *Lockit* advises him to be more
guarded, and sings the following *Air,*
　　When you censure the Age,
　　　Be cautious *and* sage,
　Lest the Courtiers *offended should be*;
　　If you mention Vice *or* Bribe,
　　'*Tis so pat to* all the Tribe,
Each cries ———*that was level'd at me.*
　　　　G 2　　　　　　　I 34

---

28. *say as much*: II.i.
29. *other People*: III.xiv.
30. *of the G_t*: Government.II.x.
31. *for it*: II.x.
32. *live besides*: II.x.
33. their Friends: II.x.
34. *at* me: Air XXX

I fubmit it, whether this is not a *plain Innuendo, that* every Courtier *is corrupted* either *with* Vice or a Bribe, *or* with Both?—For my part, if any of their *Perfons*, who are thus infamoufly treated in this Piece, will think fit to employ me, I will undertake to do them Juftice, notwithstanding the Afperfions which have been caft upon me as an Enemy to *Great Men,* and I think that I have ftill *Law* enough left to ground a *valid Information* upon it.

This is, I think, fufficient to demonftrate the *malignant Tendency* of this Piece, and of my own *good Intentions.*——*What Reafons in-*
35 *duce the G——— to be thus* paffive, *under fuch* repeated Infults, *I do not take upon me to determine.* But though I am far from wifhing, as I know it will be objected, *to* fee the *Liberty of the Stage intirely abolifhed,* yet I think fuch *licentious Invectives* on the moft *polite* and *fafhionable Vices* require fome *immediate Reftraint*; for if they continue to be allowed, the *Theatre* will become the *Cenfor* of the Age, and no Man, even of the *firft Quality* or *Diftinction,* will be at Liberty *to follow* his *Pleafures, Inclinations* or *Intereft* (which is certainly the *Birthright* of every *Free Briton*) without Danger of becoming the *May-game* of the whole Town.— I fubmit this to your fage Judgment,

And am, S I R,

Your conftant Reader and humble Servant,

Phil. Harmonicus.

---

35. *G_:* Government

92

Cooke records for us Sir Robert Walpole's attendance at a performance of the *Opera*. That he was hardly amused by being represented night after night on the stage as a criminal is also clear in Hervey's account of the notorious political suppression of *Polly*, Gay's comparatively inoffensive and far less talented sequel to the *Opera*.

William Cooke, *Memoirs of Charles Macklin, Comedian*
. . . London, 1804, pp. 53-55.

Gay . . . by frequently comparing highwaymen to courtiers, and mixing other political allusions, drew the attention of the public to the character of Sir Robert Walpole, then Prime Minister, who, like most other Prime Ministers, had a strong party against him, who constantly took care to make or find a comparison between the two characters. A particular anecdote of this nature is told of Sir Robert, which shews, what friends and enemies have long since agreed in, viz. that he possessed a fund of good humour, which could scarcely be broken in upon by any accident, with a thorough knowledge of the English character.

In the scene where Peachum and Lockit are described settling their accounts [II, x, Air XXX], Lockit sings the song,
"When you censure the age, &c."
which had such an effect on the audience, that, as if by instinct, the greater part of them threw their eyes on the stage-box, where the Minister was sitting, and loudly *encored* it. Sir Robert saw the stroke instantly, and saw it with good humour and discretion; for no sooner was the song finished, than he *encored* it a second time himself, joined in the general applause, and by this means brought the audience into so much good humour with him, that they gave him a general huzza from all parts of the house.

But, not withstanding this escape, every night, and for many years afterwards, that The Beggar's Opera was brought out, Macklin used to say, the Minister (Sir Robert Walpole) never could with any satisfaction be present at its representation, on account of the many allusions which the audience thought referred to his character. The first song [I.i. Air I] was thought to point to him— The name of *Bob Booty*, whenever mentioned [I. iii. & iv.], again raised the laugh against him: and the quarrelling scene between Peachum and Lockit [II.x.] was so well understood at that time to allude to a recent quarrel between the two Ministers, Lord Townshend and Sir Robert, that the House was in convulsions of applause.

John, Lord Hervey, *Some Materials Towards Memoirs of the Reign of King George II* (London, 1931), I, 98.

One Gay, a poet, had written a ballad opera, which was thought to reflect a little upon the court, and a good deal upon the Minister. It was called *The Beggar's Opera* . . . and was so extremely pretty in its kind that even those who were most glanced at in the satire had prudence enough to disguise their resentment by chiming in with the universal applause with which it was performed. Gay, who had attached himself to Mrs. Howard[1] and been disappointed of preferment at court, finding this couched satire upon those to whom he imputed his disappointment succeed so well, wrote a second part to this opera,[2] less pretty, but more abusive, and so little disguised, that Sir Robert Walpole resolved, rather than suffer himself to be produced for thirty nights together upon the stage in the person of a highwayman, to make use of his friend the Duke of Grafton's authority as Lord Chamberlain to put a stop to the representation of it. Accordingly this theatrical Craftsman[3] was prohibited at every playhouse.

---

1. Henrietta Howard, Countess of Suffolk, mistress of the King and therefore disliked by the Queen; she had a major influence on Court appointments.
2. *Polly*
3. *Polly* is called "this theatrical Craftsman" because, like the newspaper of that title, it satirized Walpole

IV. Opera and Music

The Beggar, who speaks for Gay, jokingly apologizes in the Introduction for the Opera's form, admitting it is not an opera "like those in vogue" because it has no "Recitative." With this exception (which saves his *Opera* from being called "unnatural") it "must be allowed an Opera in all its forms." Gay, who knew very well both Italian and English opera (he wrote the libretto for Handel's *Acis and Galatea* in 1719 or 1720), is not speaking idly here: the *Opera* does deliberately preserve most of the essential characteristics (except the recitative) of Italian opera, which is the target of the Beggar's little joke. In Gay's time those opposed to Italian opera (many, it seems, for patriotic reasons) argued that it was "unnatural," especially in its use of recitative.

What Gay creates in *his* opera is a parody, light-hearted and not at all vicious, of the Italian opera form, complete with all its excesses, including the egocentric passions of the imported Italian prima donnas who performed it. For several years the two leading prima donnas in London, Francesca Cuzzoni and Faustina Bordoni, had carried on a much-publicized feud. The rivalry between them came to a head in 1727, when, to the delight of the audience, they fought each other on stage, scratching and pulling each other's hair. Lucy, passionate and jealous, is similar to the historical Cuzzoni; Polly, modest and sincere, is roughly to be equated with Faustina. Lucy and Polly are Gay's versions of the prima donna, and whenever they face each other, there is probably some veiled burleque involved, such as in II.xiii. or III.viii. Probaby the Beggar alludes to this quarrel in the Introduction: "I have observ'd such a nice impartiality to our two ladies, that it is impossible for either of them to take offense."

There are other slight parodic touches. Lucy' speech at the beginning of III. vii. is a close counterpart in English of contemporary Italian operatic recitative.[1] The "Similes that are in all your celebrated *Operas*," according to the Beggar, can be found in Gay's lyrics. Macheath appearing in chains in Newgate is a parody of comparable operatic prison scenes (as in Handel's *Floridante* [1721]). And Gay observes, with immense irony, the happy ending that some audiences insisted on. Above all, his use of simple ballads pricked the Italian form where it was most vulnerable: in its elaborate arias and offensively artificial recitative.

James Ralph's essay in *The Touchstone* summarizes the contemporary debate about Italian opera.

---

1. Bertrand H. Bronson, "The Beggar's Opera," in *Studies in the Comic (University of California Publications in English*, Vol. VIII, No. 2, 1941) reprinted in John Loftis, ed., *Restoration Drama: Modern Essays in Criticism* (New York: Oxford University Press, 1966), p. 307.

them up to that high Pitch they now shine tri-
umphant in; and, we may boldly say, we excel
any thing *Italy* ever knew, (as to one particular
Stage) both in Composition and Performance:
For several Years they have kept their Ground,
against all vain Attempts to dislodge them; only
allowing for some small Recesses for breathing
Time; And as an *Italian* Opera can never touch
the Comprehension of above one Part in four of
a *British* Audience, it is very probable their Theatre will be crowded as long as we are a Nation.

B U T since the bare Name of an *Italian* Opera,
as established at present amongst us, is to the last
Degree shocking to the Ears of many honest Inhabitants of this M E T R O P O L I S. In order to
remove all groundless Prejudices, let us briefly
and impartially, as possible, state the Case betwixt
the contending Parties, by considering the most
material Objections to this Entertainment, and
framing a just Method of answering them Thus
wipe off, or at least compound for, those things
they look upon as Absurdities or Impositions.

I think the Objections of greatest Weight may
be reduced to four Heads. The first exclaims a-
gainst an Opera's being performed in a Language
so little understood. Its Enemies cry out against
this as a thing highly unnatural —— *What! be at-
tentive to what is* Gibberish *to us!* ——. *Chat-
t'ring Monkies!* —— *Ridiculous Apes! We spend our
Money and lose our Time, and perhaps only to be
cursed or laughed at!* —— The second is started by
those who are charmed with the M U S I C K; particularly the Airs; but nauseate the odious *Recitative:* —— Or that the Whole of an Opera should
be sung —— *They die with Laughing to hear a Ty-
rant rage and storm in a vast Regularity of Sounds;
a General sing at the Head of an Army; or a Lover,
Swan-like, expire at his Mistress's Feet; and that*
there

James Ralph, "Of Musick," in The Touchstone: Or, Historical, Critical, Political, Philosophical, and Theological Essays on the reigning Diversions of the Town . . . London: Printed, and sold by the Booksellers of London and Westminster. 1728. Pp. 12-19

there is not an imperial Mandate, a Word of Command, or Billet-doux delivered but in expressive Flats and Sharps. The third bears hard with a most general Out-cry upon the exorbitant Prices we pay the Performers; especially the Foreigners: *---Intolerable! --- so many Hundreds !--- for a Thing of nothing ! ---- a Voice ! --- a meer ha, ha ! --- nasty Pusses, odious filthy Things ! --- Let them stay at home and starve, or sing at reasonable Rates.----* The fourth is altogether critical, and raised by those Gentlemen who are Masters of so much good Sense, and just Criticism, that they are obliged to be displeased with every thing that will not stand the Test of ARISTOTLE and RAPIN. An Opera throws them into Convulsions; *one Part is ridiculous, another improbable; a third unnatural; a fourth improper; a fifth irregular,---- and so they run themselves out of Breath---- Zounds, no Unity in Time, Place or Action observed!*

LET me now, as briefly as I stated these Objections, animadvert upon them, according to the Sentiments of those who are professed Admirers of our present OPERAS: Then I shall naturally throw in my private Opinion, and, like a true Critick, point out both Beauties and Blemishes, stand up in Defence of what is right, and propose Remedies for what is wrong.

As to the first Objection; The musical Part of this and all other modern Nations have agreed, that the *Italian* is undoubtedly the most proper Language to be joined to Sounds, for Reasons so obvious, that it would be Impertinence to mention them. But, not to tire my Reader with Quotations, let us hear what one of our greatest Refiners and Improvers of the *English* Tongue says; and every Man will allow DRYDEN to be a Judge: *All, says he, who are conversant in that noble Language,*

C

the

---

1. *Billet-doux*: love letter
2. Rapin: influential 17th century French neo-classical critic

the Italian, *cannot but obferve, that it is the fofteft, fweeteft, and moft harmonious, not only of any modern Tongue, but even beyond any of the Learned. It feems to have been invented not only for* POETRY, *but* MUSICK; *the Vowels fo abounding in all Words, efpecially in the Terminations, that, excepting a few Monofyllables, the whole Language ends in them. Then their Pronunciation is fo fonorous, that their very Speaking has more* MUSICK *in it, than* Dutch POETRY *and* SONG: *And if we muft call it barbarous, it is the moft beautiful and moft learned*
3 *of any* Barbarifm *in the modern Tongues.*

IN the next place we cannot have native Performers for our Mother Tongue, but what will fall far fhort of the excellent Voices and Tafte of thofe we are fupplied with from Abroad: Some Women we boaft of, and Boys; but the firft generally lofe their Voices before they begin to learn, and are then ill taught; as the latter are obliged by Nature to part with theirs, by the time they know any thing of the Matter: A tolerable Bafs Voice we may meet with by Chance in an Age: But as we are denied the Liberty of artificially tuning the Pipes of thofe Performers who are neither Men nor Women, and who are the Foundation of the *Italian* OPERAS; I do aver, that I think it impoffible to form a perfect and compleat Mufical Entertainment of our own People, or in our own Language.

NOT to go any farther back than laft Winter, the Attempt of introducing *Englifh* Operas at
4 *L——n's-Inn-F——ds* Theatre, will fufficiently juftifie my Affertion. Their Endeavours, though headed by a great Mafter, and fupported by fome People of the beft Fafhion and Intereft, in a few Weeks did but expofe to the Ridicule of every body, that had any Notion of MUSICK, their wretched

---

3. *Tongues:* Preface to *Albion and Albanius* (*Essays of John Dryden*, ed. W. P. Ker, I, 273-4)
4. *L_n's-Inn-F_ds* Theatre: Lincoln's Inn Fields

ed Performance; and even then, thofe that made the beft Figure on their Stage were Foreigners: 'Tis true, that Reprefentation had a Run, (as they term it) and brought feveral full Houfes; but I fpeak of its Merit, and not its Succefs; the firft was obvious to every Ear; the laft was forced by a Party, during the Vacation of the *Italian* OPERAS.

NOTHING but the Wantonnefs of Plenty from the loweft Neceffity, could have thrown People into fuch an Abfurdity, thus profufely to fquander away on bad Voices, what was got by clever Heels; and to choofe that Seafon, when the whole of *Englifh* MUSICK was at the loweft Ebb, and the OPERAS at the *H—y-M—t* at 5 that Height, (both as to Compofition and Performance) which no ancient Theatre could ever have an Idea of; nay, it is almoft unknown to *Italy* it felf.

I was fo unfortunate, as to be oblig'd once to fit *Ca —— la* out, to the great Difquiet of my Ears; 6 nor have I perfectly got rid of the Head-ach it gave me, yet; and I vow, had it not been for Mrs. *B —— ier,* and my old Friend *L —— dge,* I 7, 8 could have fwore the Stage had returned the Favour the Audience fometimes does them, and play'd a full Choir of Cat-calls upon us.

THIS Seafon they reviv'd *Thomyris* at *L——n's* 9 *Inn-F——ds*; but that being rather a better OPERA, and more juftly performed than the other, the Town would not go near it.

So finding their Finances run very low, by ftriving to do well, they thought it abfolutely neceffary to do fomething very bad, in order to retrieve their undone Affairs.

THIS indeed they have happily effected in Conjunction with a great Poet; and by giving us

C 2 fome-

---

5. *H_y M_t*: Haymarket, the London theatre where the Italian opera was performed
6. *Ca_la*: Camilla (1706), opera with music by Buononcini, adapted by Haym, frequently performed
7. Mrs. *B_ier*: Jane Barbier, d. 1757, opera singer, she sang in *Camilla* in 1717 and 1726-27.
8. *L_dge*: Richard Loveridge, 1670?-1758, vocalist, song-writer, composer; he sang in *Camilla*
9. *Thomyris*: *Thomyris, Queen of Scythia*, an opera with music by Scarlatti and Buononcini, adapted by Pepusch

fomething more execrable in relation to MUSICK, than the World ever dreamt of feeing on any Stage, they are Made; and we run mad with Joy in being fo agreeably difappointed.

THE *Beggar's Opera*, by robbing the Performers at *Pye-corner*, *Fleet-ditch*, *Moor-fields* (and other Stations of this Metropolis, famed for travelling Sounds) of their undoubted Properties, has reinftated them in Wealth and Grandeur; and what fhock'd moft Ears, and fet moft Teeth on edge, at turning the Corner of a Street, for half a Moment; when thrown into a regular Entertainment, charms for Hours.

I muft own they never appear'd to that Advantage in any mufical Light as this OPERA of *Beggars*: Their Rags of POETRY and Scraps of MUSICK joining fo naturally, that in whatever View we confider it as to Character or Circumftance, its Title is the moft *apropos* Thought upon Earth.

THE fecond Objection, at firft Sight, may appear very plaufible; but, upon Examination, very ill grounded; for it is impoffible to have a perfect mufical *Dramma*, without Recitative: No Ear can fupport the Whole being all Air; therefore if you take away the Recitative, it is no OPERA: And the beft Judges value a Mafter as much upon the Merit of one as the other: The Recitative is but a tuneable Method of fpeaking; and in the Article of MUSICK, but refines upon Speech, as far as polite Comedy excels common Converfation, or Tragedy in Heroicks, the ordinary Stile of the Great. As for the critical Part of the Objection againft Recitative, I defire that our Poets, Criticks, and Fine Gentlemen, banifh firft greater Abfurdities and Inconfiftencies from their Stage-Plays; for I
cannot

cannot imagine, that to fing all the Parts of an OPERA is by half fo unnatural, as the fparkling Nonfenfe, gilded Fuftian, and pompous Bombaft in moft, if not all our Tragedies; nor fo improper as the quaint *Double Entendres,* and forc'd Similies, fqueez'd out in the midft of Misfortunes, or at the Point of Death: The Heroes there quietly and ftupidly fleep over four Acts in a dull regular Way of Life, till by Danger they are rouz'd from their Lethargy into a State of Wit; like the Prince born dumb, whofe Tongue was never loofen'd, till the Sword was at his Father's Throat. In fhort, nothing is ridiculous that executes a regular Defign: That of an OPERA, is to reprefent to us, in the Drammatick Way, fome inftructive *Fable,* where the Words are all to be deliver'd in MUSICK; therefore a King muft rule, a General fight, a Lover figh, in Harmony: Nor is there wanting in this Art a Variety to touch the different Paffions, as juftly as any Kind of POETRY: Nor can I obferve any thing in finging a Converfation - Piece, more abfurd or ridiculous than a familiar Dialogue in Heroick *Rhime.*

THE third Objection indeed carries great Weight with it: Our Prices are immoderately extravagant; and all we can fay to juftify them is, that we are arrived now to fo picquant a *Gou* 10 in MUSICK, that nothing but what is fuperexcellent will pafs. What pleafes at *Venice* or *Rome* may chance to be hifs'd at the *H---y-M--t.* If we muft have thofe of the greateft Merit, they will be paid accordingly. If they don't meet with more Encouragement here than at Home, who will run the Hazard of coming near us? Should we pay them double, ftill the Odds is againft them; an Englifh Morning or Evening

C 3   may

---

10. *Gou: goût, taste*

may ruin them for ever, and a North-Eaſt Blaſt in *July* rob them of their Bread at once: 'Tis but juſt, that if our Ears demand the beſt Performers, that our Purſes ſhould pay the higheſt Prices; elſe 'tis culling the choiceſt Fruit at *Leaden-Hall* and *Covent-Garden* Markets, and expect it as cheap as the withered Refuſe of a blind Alley-Stall.

THE exorbitant Expences occaſion'd by introducing an *Italian* OPERA amongſt us, may be reduc'd to two Heads: *Firſt*, the vaſt Salaries given to the Singers by the Academy. *Secondly*, what the Audience pays to the Academy, which is the natural Conſequence of the other. As to the firſt, I think it fully anſwer'd before, nor is the Academy in the leaſt to blame; our Taſte is ſo refin'd, and our Judgment ſo ſolid in relation to all Parts of MUSICK, that ſuch an Entertainment cannot be ſupported but by the Tip-top Performers of the World; and they will have Prices equal to their Merit. As to the ſecond, it would be highly unreaſonable to expect that the Directors of the *H——y-M——t* Th——re ſhould amuſe us at their own private Expence; they run a great Riſque to pleaſe us, in engaging for vaſt Sums, whilſt it is left to our Choice whether we'll come or no, to eaſe them of Part of the Burden: Nor can they with the higheſt Prices be certain of coming off clear one Seaſon, unleſs they have crowded Houſes every Night.

THE fourth Objection is altogether critical, and carry'd on in the ſtiff pedantick Rules that Tribe have ſettled, by which they form a Judgment on every thing polite, and of conſequence damn all Amuſements where Spirit and Life prevail over their unanimated Works of Clay. Theſe merry Gentlemen would reduce OPERAS to the

Standard

11. the Academy: the Royal Academy of Music which sponsored the Italian opera

Standard of *Ariſtotle* and *Rapin*. Should theſe Entertainments in any Point prove Malefactors, they
are for bringing them before improper Judges;
it is carrying the Cauſe into as wrong a Court
of Judicature, as trying a Pyrate for Murder in
Chancery, or a Highwayman in *Doctors-Commons*. 12,13
An OPERA borrows no Helps from their *Poe-*
ticks, is not built upon the Foundation of their
Stages, nor muſt their Rules interfere with any
Part of the Superſtructure : Were it otherways,
why ſhould not this Amuſement as well as others,
upon Occaſion, plead the Benefit of their Clergy;
and when it is guilty of what is irregular or unnatural, excuſe it, by calling it a bright Thought
and bold Beauty. It has ever been granted by
thoſe who allow an OPERA any Exiſtence at all,
that things wholly ſuper-natural and marvellous
are warrantable in this Kind of *Dramma*; though
they would be damn'd in a regular Tragedy or
Comedy : AN OPERA may be be call'd the Ty-
rant of the Stage; it is ſubject to no poetical
Laws, deſpiſes the Power or Limitations of a Parliament of Criticks; and ſubſiſts altogether by
abſolute Sway, and its own uucontroulable Pre-
rogative : It has Liberty to range Heaven, Earth,
and Hell; call Gods, Spirits, and Devils to its
Aſſiſtance; and all this unbounded Freedom is
taken for the Probable, or rather what is neceſſary in this Entertainment.

---

12. *Chancery*: the court of equity
13. *Doctors-Commons*: courts largely concerned with the registration or probate of
    wills, marriage licenses, and proceedings for divorce

Much of the incontestable attractiveness of *The Beggar's Opera* comes from its ballad airs and the charming lyrics Gay wrote for them. Out of the sixty-nine airs in the *Opera* forty-one were derived from the tunes of broadside ballads. Such ballads were short songs, lyrical or narrative, set to well-known tunes and commonly sold up and down the streets. Familiar to all, these tunes were a deeply loved part of England's musical heritage.

The broadside words were usually topical, satirical, or political: "A New Ballad to the Tune of _." Printed on single sheets they were sung and sold by ballad-singers, who were often professional beggars. The Beggar, in the Introduction, admits his piece was "originally writ for the celebrating the marriage of *James Chanter* and *Moll Lay,* two most excellent ballad-singers." Gay's innovative idea was to bring ballad airs into the theatre from the streets and give them new words.

His primary source for the ballad tunes was a famous six-volume collection of Thomas D'Urfey's, *Pills To Purge Melancholy.* For the rest of his tunes, Gay relied on some of the best known composers of his day. Henry Purcell, the great seventeenth-century baroque composer, is used most frequently, followed by Handel, Buononcini, and Sandoni, all opera composers working in England during Gay's time.

Since we have the original words of the airs that Gay adapted, it is possible to recapture an important contemporary appreciation. Though sometimes he simply set new words to the old tune, with minimal allusion to the original words, he often deliberately exploited the fact that his audience knew the original words by heart. Between the new words and those originally sung to that air, Gay intends an ironic contrast which makes an important part of the dramatic effect.

Gay's Air IV, "If Love the virgin's heart invade," warns against seduction and the danger of the virgin's becoming "what I dare not name." The original song, "Why is your faithful Slave disdain'd." urges quite the contrary—the lover here begs his mistress to allow him to possess what he dares not name. Polly's moving "Virgins are like the fair flower" (Air VI) with its brutal ending in Covent Garden (famous for produce and prostitutes) gains in bitterness from being heard against the luscious "What shall I do to show how much I love her," where the lover, much concerned with his performance, dies a glorious sexual death:

In fair *Aurelia*'s Arms, leave me expiring,
    To be Imbalm'd with the sweets of her Breath;
To the last moment I'll still be desiring;
    Never had Hero so glorious a Death.

Compare these words to Polly's comments on defloration:

But, when once pluck'd, 'tis no longer alluring,
    To *Covent-Garden* 'tis sent; (as yet sweet)
There fades, and shrinks, and grows past all enduring,
    Rots, stinks, and dies, and is trod under feet.

In Air IX Gay juxtaposes Mrs. Peachum's dubious advice with that of the moral Molly's in "Oh Jenny, Jenny, where hast thou been?" Likewise, he sets off the gay amorousness of Macheath's "If the heart of a man is deprest with cares" (Air XXI) by using the tune of a three-stanza manual of seduction, "Would ye have a young Virgin of fifteen Years?"

Wit and Mirth: Or, Pills To Purge Melancholy: Being A Collection of the best Merry Ballads and Songs, Old and New . . . [6 vols.] The Fourth Edition . . . London: Printed by W. Pearson, for J. Tonson, at Shake-spear's Head, over-against Catherine Street in the Strand, 1719.

The Farmer's *Daughter:* A SONG.

COLD and Raw the North did blow,
  Bleak in the Morning early ;
All the Trees were hid in Snow,
  Dagl'd by Winter yearly :
When come Riding over a Knough,
  I met with a Farmer's Daughter ;
Rofie Cheeks and bonny Brow,
  Good faith made my Mouth to water.

Down I vail'd my Bonnet low,
  Meaning to fhew my breeding ;
She return'd a graceful bow,
  A Vifage far exceeding:

"The Farmer's Daughter" ["Cold and Raw], II, 167-68. Gay's Air III, "If
any wench Venus's girdle wear"

I ask'd her where she went so soon,
　　And long'd to begin a Parly;
She told me unto the next Market Town,
　　A purpose to sell her Barly.

In this purse, sweet Soul, said I,
　　Twenty pounds lie fairly;
Seek no farther one to buy,
　　For I'se take all thy Barly:
Twenty more shall buy Delight,
　　Thy Person I Love so dearly;
If thou wouldst stay with me all Night,
　　And go home in the Morning early.

If Twenty pound could buy the Globe,
　　Quoth she, this I'd not do, Sir;
Or were my Kin as poor as *Job*,
　　I wo'd not raise 'em so, Sir:
For should I be to Night your friend,
　　We'st get a young Kid together;
And you'd be gone ere the nine Months end,
　　And where should I find a Father?

I told her I had Wedded been,
　　Fourteen years and longer;
Or else I choose her for my Queen,
　　And tie the Knot much stronger:
She bid me then no farther rome,
　　But manage my Wedlock fairly;
And keep Purse for poor Spouse at home,
　　For some other shall have her Barly.

A SONG.

WHY is your faithful Slave difdain'd?
By gentle Arts my Heart you gain'd!
Oh, keep it by the fame!
For ever fhall my Paffion laft,
If you will make me once poffeft,
Of what I dare not name.

Tho' charming are your Wit and Face,
'Tis not alone to hear and gaze,
That will fuffice my Flame ;
Love's Infancy on Hopes may live,
But you to mine full grown muft give,
Of what I dare not name.

When

"Why is your faithful Slave disdain'd", III, 211-212. Gay's Air IV, "If love
the virgin's heart invade"

When I behold your Lips, your Eyes,
Thoſe ſnowy Breaſts that fall and riſe,
    Fanning my raging Flame;
That Shape ſo made to be imbrac't,
What would I give I might but taſte,
    Of what I dare not name!

In Courts I never wiſh to riſe,
Both Wealth and Honour I deſpiſe,
    And that vain Breath call'd Fame;
By Love, I hope no Crowns to gain,
'Tis ſomething more I would obtain,
    'Tis that I dare not name.

WHat fhall I do to fhew how much I love her,
    How many Millions of Sighs can fuffice?
That which wins other Hearts ne'er can move her,
    Thofe common methods of Love fhe'll defpife:
I will love more than Man e'er lov'd before me,
    Gaze on her all the Day, and melt all the Night,
'Till for her own fake at laft fhe'll implore me,
    To Love her lefs to preferve our delight.

Since Gods themfelves could not ever be Loving,
    Men muft have breathing Recruits for new Joys;
I wifh my Soul could be ever improving,
    Tho' eager Love, more than forrow deftroys.
In fair *Aurelia's* Arms, leave me expiring,
    To be Imbalm'd with the fweets of her Breath;
To the laft moment I'll ftill be defiring;
    Never had Hero fo glorious a Death.

"What shall I do to show how much I love her", IV, 235. Gay's Air VI,
"Virgins are like the fair flower in its lustre"

113

The Willoughby WHIM.

A Scotch SONG.

In a DIALOGUE *between two Sisters.*

Molly. OH *Jenny, Jenny,* where haft thou been?
Father and Mother are feeking for thee,
You have been ranting, playing the Wanton,
Keeping of *Jockey* Company.

Jenny. Oh *Molly,* I've been to hear Mill clack,
And grind Grift for the Family,
Full as it went I've brought home my Sack,
For the Miller has tooken his Toll of me.

Molly. You hang your Smickets abroad to bleach,
When that was done, where could you be?
Jenny I flipt down in the quickfet Hedge,
And *Jockey* the Loon fell after me.

Molly. My Father you told you'd go to Kirk,
When Prayers were done, where could you be?
Jenny. Taking a Kifs of the Parfon and Clerk,
And of other young Laddys fome two or three.

Molly. Oh *Jenny, Jenny,* what wilt thou do,
If Belly fhould fwell, where wilt thou be?
Jenny. Look to your felf for *Jockey* is true,
And whilft Clapper goes will take care of me.

I   *The*

"The Willoughby Whim". A Scotch Song, ["Oh, Jenny, Jenny"], I, 169.
Gay's Air IX, "O Polly, you might have toy'd and kist"

114

WOuld ye have a young Virgin of fifteen Years,
    You muſt tickle her Fancy with ſweets and dears,
Ever toying, and playing, and ſweetly, ſweetly,
Sing a Love Sonnet, and charm her Ears:
Wittily, prettily talk her down,
Chaſe her, and praiſe her, if fair or brown,
        Sooth her, and ſmooth her,
        And teaze her, and pleaſe her,
And touch but her Smicket, and all's your own.

Do ye fancy a Widow well known in a Man?
With a front of Aſſurance come boldly on,
Let her reſt not an Hour, but briskly, briskly,
Put her in mind how her Time ſteals on;
Rattle and prattle although ſhe frown,
Rowſe her, and towſe her from Morn to Noon,
Shew her ſome Hour y'are able to grapple,
Then get but her Writings, and all's your own.

Do ye fancy a Punk of a Humour free,
That's kept by a Fumbler of Quality,
You muſt rail at her Keeper, and tell her, tell her
        Pleaſure's beſt Charm is Variety,
Swear her much fairer than all the Town,
Try her, and ply her when Cully's gone,
        Dog her, and jog her,
        And meet her, and treat her,
And kiſs with two Guinea's, and all's your o¹

"Would ye have a young Virgin of fifteen Years", I, 133. Gay's Air XXI,
"If the heart of a man is deprest with cares"

Lumps of PUDDING.

WHEN I was in the low Country,
    When I was in the low Country;
What flices of Pudding and pieces of Bread,
My Mother gave me when I was in need. ·

My Mother fhe kill'd a good fat Hog,
She made fuch Puddings would choak a Dog;
And I fhall ne'er forget 'till I dee,
What lumps of Pudding my Mother gave me.

She hung them up upon a Pin,
The Fat run out and the Maggots crept in;
If you won't believe me you may go and fee,
    What lumps, *&c.*

And every Day my Mother would cry,
Come ftuff your Belly Girl until you die;
'Twou'd make you to laugh if you were to fee,
    What lumps, *&c.*

I no fooner at Night was got into Bed,
But fhe all in kindnefs would come with fpeed;
She gave me fuch parcels I thought I fhould dee,
    With eating of Pudding, *&c.*   **At**

"Lumps of Pudding," VI, 300-01. Gay's Air LXIX, "Thus I stand like
a Turk, with his doxies around"

At laft I Rambled abroad and then,
I met in my Frolick an honeft Man;
Quoth he my dear *Philli* I'll give unto thee,
Such Pudding you never did fee.

Said I honeft Man, I thank thee moft kind,
And as he told me indeed I did find;
He gave me a lump which did fo agree,
One bit was worth all my Mother gave me.

V. The Morality Problem

Hardly a month after its first performance, worried moralists began protesting against the pernicious influence of *The Beggar's Opera*. In March 1728 Dr. Thomas Herring, King's Chaplain and later Archbishop of York and Canterbury, preached a sermon against it in Lincoln's Inn Chapel. The sermon, which has not survived, was apparently much talked of. Gay writing to Swift sounds amused: "I suppose you must have heard that I have had the honour to have had a Sermon preach'd against my works by a Court Chaplain, which I look upon as so small addition to my fame."[1]

The "morality problem" is less naive than it might at first seem. We are still not sure today what exactly our response to Macheath should be. Though the polical references have faded, Gay's vision remains disturbingly anarchic. We reprint an account of the lost sermon by Herring's editor, William Duncombe. We also reprint a selection from *Thievery A-la-mode: Or The Fatal Encouragement*, a crude melodramatic novel that shows the interpretation given Gay's themes. Before our selection opens, the hero, Millefont, has been left in dire poverty with his two sisters, by the death of his father.

Gay's great friend, Jonathan Swift, who was as well Dean of the Anglican Cathedral in Dublin, came to the defense of the *Opera* in the third issue of *The Intelligencer*. His essay on it is not only a defense of its morality (Swift was, of course, interested in proving that anti-Walpole satire was not immoral) but the best contemporary criticism we have on the central meaning of the play.

Boswell's attitude to the morality problem is typically ambivalent, and Johnson's judgment is the best-known and the sanest.

---

1. *The Letters of John Gay*, ed. C. F. Burgess (Oxford: Clarendon Press, 1966), Gay to Swift, 16 May 1728, p. 75.

tian Life, which are fo affectionately recommended in the Gofpel. He was of Opinion, with a very inge- nious Writer, that "true Religion "is true Reafon, which fmiles at "pointed Wit, mocks the Scoffer's "Tongue, and is alike invulne- "rable by Ridicule or Rage."

Once indeed a great Clamour was raifed on account of his allud- ing to a popular Entertainment, then exhibited at the neighbouring Theatre, and prefuming to con- demn it, as of pernicious Confe- quence in regard to the Practice of Morality and Chriftian Virtue. He was not fingular in this Opi- nion ; and Experience afterwards confirmed the Truth of his Obfer- vations, fince feveral Thieves and Street-robbers confeffed in *New-* [1] *gate,* that they raifed their Cou- rage at the Playhoufe, by the Songs

a 3 of

The Preface to: Seven Sermons On Public Occasions. By the Most Reverend Dr. Thomas Herring [edited by William Duncombe] . . . London: Printed for the Editor, 1763. Pp. v-x.

1. *Newgate*: London prison

of their Hero *Macheath*, before they fallied forth on their defperate nocturnal Exploits.

As it may be prefumed that Prejudice is hufhed by Length of Time, and the ftill Voice of Reafon will probably now be heard, we will lay before the Reader Two Letters, in Juftification of the Doctrine maintained in that Sermon, which were then printed, on different Days, in one of the weekly Papers.

—— *Non fi quid turbida Roma*
2   *Elevet, accedas.*   PERSIUS.

" *S I R,*   *March* 30, 1728.

" IT has, I think, been generally
" agreed among Moralifts, that
" all public Sports and Entertain-
" ments fhould be fo regulated, as
" to have a Tendency to the En-
" couragement of Virtue, and the
                          " difcoun-

---

2. *accedas:* 'You do not go along if disordered Rome elevates something of little
     worth; Persius, I.5-6

" difcountenancing of Vice and Im-
" morality. The Practice eftablifhed
" by the wifeft Legiflators, who were
" fenfible how great an Influence
" Plays and other Diverfions have
" on the Minds of the Populace,
" has been conformable to this falu-
" tary Maxim. How fhocking then
" would it have appeared to the
" venerable Sages of Antiquity, to
" have feen an Author bring upon
" the Stage, as a proper Subject for
" Laughter and Merriment, a Gang
" of Highwaymen and Pickpockets
" triumphing in their fuccefsful Vil-
" lainies, and braving the ignomi-
" nious Death they fo juftly deferve,
" with the undaunted Refolution of
" a *Stoic* Philofopher? The Courage
" expreffed in the following Lines
" would have become a *Seneca* or a 3
" *Raleigh*, but feems not fo fuitable 4
" to the Character of a Criminal.

a 4   " *The*

---

3. *Seneca*: c.4 B.C.-A.D.65, Roman stoic whose fortitude in committing suicide
   became legendary
4. *Raleigh*: Sir Walter Raleigh, who faced his execution with serenity

" *The Charge is prepar'd; the Lawyers are met;*
   " *The Judges all rang'd (a terrible Show!)*
  " *I go undismay'd——for Death is a Debt,*
5   " *A Debt on Demand——so, take what I owe.*

    " The chief End of Punifhment
    " is to prevent the Commiffion of
    " the like Offences for the future;
    " and therefore all good Subjects
    " fhould endeavour, as far as they
    " are able, to heighten the Terror
    " of the Penalties annexed by the
    " Laws to flagrant Crimes: But to
    " place (on the contrary) thefe Pe-
    " nalties in a ludicrous Light, and
    " to reprefent them as eafy to be
    " borne, and contemptible, is, in
    " effect, blunting the Edge of the
    " Civil Sword, and opening the
    " Flood-Gates (if I may fo fpeak)
    " to the moft outrageous Enormi-
    " ties. The Mifchief will be ftill
    " farther promoted, if the Lives of
    " fuch abandoned Wretches as Rob-
                        " bers

---

5. *what I owe*: Air LVII

" bers and Street-walkers, are de-
" fcribed as agreeable, and full of
" Mirth and Pleafure.   How far a
" late celebrated Entertainment may
" have contributed towards thofe
" daring Attacks, which are daily
" committed on the Property of
" the Subject in the Streets of our
" Capital (in Defiance of all Law,
" and, I believe, beyond the Exam-
" ple of former Ages), I will not
" pretend to fay; but, I am fure,
" nothing can be more proper to
" foment thefe Violences than fuch
" Lines as thefe;

> " *See the Ball I hold!*
> " *Let the Chymifts toil like Affes,*
> " *Our Fire their Fire furpaffes,*
> " *And turns all our Lead to Gold.*   6

" The Agreeablenefs of the En-
" tertainment, and its being adapted
" to the Tafte of the Vulgar, and
                    8   " fet

---

6. *Lead to Gold*: Air XX

" fet to eafy Tunes (which almoft
" every-body can remember), makes
" the Contagion fpread wider, and
" the Confequence the more to be
" dreaded.

with that Kinfwoman who had at firft taken
her into her Charge ; but that Lady being
now of a great Age, her Death was every
day expected, and the beft part of her In-
come dying with herfelf, there was little to
be hoped from her Children, who would
have barely fufficient to fupport themfelves
in the manner they had been educated.
The fevereft weight of Woe now lay on
Millefont ; the Apprehenfions of what he
was in all probability to fuffer himfelf,
were nothing to the Anguifh he fuftain'd on
the account of thefe unhappy Girls, the
Delicacy of their Sex rendering them lefs
able to fuftain the Hardfhips of Want, and
their Beauty filling him with continual
Terrors, that fome time or other that
might betray them to a worfe Ill than Poverty.

While he was taken up with thefe diftrac-
ting Meditations, a young Gentleman of his
Acquaintance, who was alfo his Friend as
far as a Bottle of Wine, or a Supper,
would needs have him go with him to a
whimfical Entertainment at the Play-Houfe,
very much in vogue, call'd the *Beggar's
Opera*. The Houfe was fo extremely full,
that tho' they went at four o'clock, they
could get no Seat, but were obliged to ftand

C 2   at

Thievery A-la-mode; Or The Fatal Encouragement . . . London: Printed
for J. Roberts, near the Oxford-Arms in Warwick-Lane, 1728; Pp. 11-27;
pp. 1-11 omitted.

at the Pit-door. *Millefont,* whofe Soul
at prefent was little tun'd for fuch Diverfions, would fain have perfuaded his Friend
to go out; but the other cry'd out on his
ill Tafte; fwore that no Fatigue was too
great for the Pleafure they fhould receive
when the Actors fhould begin; adding, that
he had been a Spectator of the fame Entertainment for two and thirty Nights, yet ftill
came to it with more than the Raptures of
a firft Enjoyment of a Miftrefs. Their
Converfation happening to be pretty loud,
feveral Gentlemen that fat near, join'd
with him in opinion, faying, nothing was
ever fo agreeable; one protefting, that
he had feen it five and thirty times, another
forty; and a third, that he had not mifs'd
once the Reprefentation of it, nor would,
if it lafted the whole Seafon, which he
heartily wifh'd it might. Such prodigious
Encomiums, given by Perfons who feem'd
to be of diftinction, and had good Senfe,
made *Millefont* more patiently endure the
little Eafe of his Situation; but ftrangely
was he amaz'd, when the opening Scenes
prefented only Characters, which to him
feem'd too low to afford any Pleafure to an
elegant Tafte. He underftood the thing,
as certainly it was intended by the Author,
a Satyr on the Inconfiftencies and unnatural
Con-

Conduct of the *Italian Operas*, which, tho' they charm the Eye with gay Dreſſes, and fine Scenes, and delight the Ear with Sound, have nothing in them either to reform the Manners, or improve the Mind, the original Inſtitution of the Stage. But he found few who thought as he did; they did not ſeem to take the Meaning of the Poet; they admir'd it for the Whim, and becauſe it made them laugh, but had not at all the worſe Opinion of thoſe Performances it was deſign'd to ridicule: And this Obſervation threw him into very ſerious Reflections on the capricious Diſpoſition of the Age.

Some few days after, paſſing by a great Picture-ſhop, he ſaw the Prints of Captain *Macheath* and *Polly Peachum* hanging in the Windows with thoſe of the firſt Quality of both Sexes in the Kingdom. And the ſame Evening happening to be at a Place where ſeveral Ladies were viſiting, he obſerved that every one of them had the agreeable Highway-man and his two Doxies 1 painted on their Fans and Snuff-boxes. What, *ſaid he to himſelf*, is it become an emulative piece of Gentility to encourage the vileſt Characters that Nature will bear? How many worthy Parts has Mr. *Walker* 2

ap-

---

1. Doxies: mistresses
2. Mr. *Walker*: the original Macheath. See 'The First Season'

appear'd in on the Stage ? How many great
Heroes have feem'd to live again in the Re-
3,4 prefentation of Mr. *Booth* and Mr. *Wilks* ?
But the Applaufe they receiv'd for them was
almoſt as ſhort-liv'd as the Performance!
The Morals of the *Patriot*, and the graceful
Geſture, and fine Utterance of the *Actor*,
were alike remember'd ! In various Scenes
Mr. *Walker* has appear'd in the moſt advan-
tageous Colours, and tho' he *merited*, never
could arrive at the Honours he now enjoys.
——Is it then to the moſt low, vicious, and
depraved Character he owes his Fame ?——
Moſt certainly ! elfe he had not fo long been
neglected.——Degenerate Age ! when only
Crimes, and thofe too of a nature which
none but the meaneſt and moſt wretched
part of the Creation can ſubmit to be
guilty of, ſhall be immortaliz'd in Paint and
Verfe.

Thus did he reafon with himfelf; and
coming out of his Soliloquy, could not forbear expreffing aloud fome part of his Sentiments; but he was prefently filenced,
over-born by a torrent of Praifes almoſt as
abfurd as the Theme they were upon. The
general Voice was againſt him, and he durſt
not infift on the Subject, for fear of being
ac-

3. Mr. *Booth:* Barton Booth, 1681-1733, actor, famous as the lead in Addison's *Cato*
4. Mr. *Wilks*: Robert Wilks, 1665?-1732, actor

accounted a Perſon entirely devoted to his own Opinion.

In fine, he could go into no Company, hear no Diſcourſe, but what was taken up with the charming Charaÿters of Captain *Macheath* and *Polly Peachum.* Surprize, they ſay, wears off, and the moſt prodigious Events, when become frequent, ceaſe to excite wonder ; yet could not his diminiſh at ſo aſtoniſhing a Proof of the Stupidity, to give it no worſe a Name, of the Town. Good God ! cry'd he, as often as any Teſtimonies of this nature reach'd his Ears, of what uſe are now the great Examples drawn from the Heroes of Antiquity, or the more lively Inſtances of the preſent Worthies ? The god-like Virtues of *Tamer-* 5 *lane* no more excite Applauſe ! *'Belliſarius* 6 mourns in vain, and the Lover of his Country, *Cato,* is forgot ! The Conqueſts of 7 our fifth *Henry!* the Piety of the ſixth ! and Valour of the fam'd *Black Prince !* 8 are Subjeÿts too dull for the modiſh Converſation of theſe Times. The Cant of *Newgate,* and that ſort of Behaviour which ſome Malefaÿtors are guilty of, even when under Condemnation, and was accuſtom'd to be ſo ſhocking to a thinking Soul, when any account happen'd to be given of it by

the

5. *Tamerlane*: 1333?-1405, the famous Mongol conqueror of most of southern and western Asia
6. *Bellisarius*: A.D.505-565, general of the Eastern Roman Empire
7. *Cato*: 95-46 B.C., Roman Stoic philosopher
8. *Black Prince*: 1330-76, Edward, Prince of Wales, son of Edward III

9 the *Ordinary*, is now a Matter of Mirth,
and charms the *British* Genius more than
10 *Shakespear*, or than *Otway* ever could.

But tho' he was not of a Difpofition
to be biafs'd by the Caprice of others a-
gainft his own Reafon, and had by Nature
and Education the utmoft abhorrence for
any thing that tended to the Encouragement
of Vice ; yet being driven to the utmoft
Defpair by the Unkindnefs of his Friends,
and the little regard he found paid to Virtue,
he at laft form'd a Refolution to have re-
courfe to what he moft hated, fince his Inclinations and Perfeverance in following the
other, afforded him no Relief.   In this
defpairing Humour, he provided himfelf of
a good Horfe and Piftols, and fet up for
Captain *Macheath*'s Profeffion ; in which
he had great Succefs, the firft day prefenting
him with a Booty of above two hundred
Pounds, befides leaving the Perfon from
whom he took it, fufficient to bear his
Charges to his Journey's end.   The next,
he met an old Change-Broker, who he
knew to be one of thofe who had affifted
in the Ruin of his Father ; from him he
got fifty Pounds : but foon after encoun-
tring a poor *Scotch* Pedlar, who had been
robb'd by two Foot-pads of his Pack and

I   Money,

---

9. *Ordinary*: the chaplain of Newgate prison, who published criminal lives
10. *Otway*: Thomas Otway, 1652-85, author of the celebrated Restoration tragedies,
    The Orphan and *Venice Preserv'd*.

Money, the Value of which, he said, was above forty Pounds; the generous *Millefont* made up his loss out of the Broker's Stock.

He had not follow'd the Road above a Week before his Courage and good Fortune made him the Master of a thousand Pounds, the most part of which he lodg'd in the Bank for the Use of his Sisters, who, amazed at this sudden Change in his Fortune, were very inquisitive into the Cause; but he refused acquainting them, fearing the knowledge of successful Vice might taint their Virtue, and encourage them also to Actions not warrantable.

Many various Adventures he met with in his new Profession in a small space of time; but they being only such as may ordinarily happen to Persons who travel on the account he did, I shall pass them over in silence, lest my Reader should imagine I design to imitate what I have condemn'd, and would entertain him with the Tricks and Dialect of a common Thief. I shall therefore only particularize one Occurrence, which I think remarkable enough to employ the Pen of a better Writer than myself.

D

Hap.

Happening to be ftroll'd farther into the Country than he had been accuftom'd, he heard at a fmall diftance a Hunting-Horn and a Pack of Dogs. That being a Diverfion he was extremely fond of, he ftop'd his Horfe a while to liften to it; but was foon rouz'd from that Amufement by the appearance of a Gentleman and a Lady, who feem'd by their Dreffes to be Hunters, but had quitted the Company for a Game they liked better. On the firft noife of their Horfes, he withdrew behind a Thicket, where, difmounting, he conceal'd himfelf the better to obferve them. The Place they were in being the Entrance of a Wood, he faw the Gentleman alight, and having help'd the Lady to do fo too, he tied the two Horfes by the Bridles to an Oak, and taking his fair Partner by the Hand, led her farther into the fhady Recefs.

Millefont perceiving this, faften'd his own Horfe, and making what hafte he could after them, overtook them juft as they were about to fit down on a fine graffy Bank at the foot of a Tree. The noife of fomebody near, made them turn haftily about, furpriz'd beyond meafure at the fight of a Man in a place where they had imagin'd them-

themfelves entirely without danger of In-
terruption of any kind whatfoever ; but
were infinitely more fo, as well as frighted,
when *Millefont*, prefenting his Piftol, bid
them deliver what they had of Value. The
Gentleman was altogether unprovided of
means of refiftance, and therefore defiring
him not to fright the Lady, was preparing
to pluck out his Watch and Money, making an excufe that he had but little, it being Pleafure only that had drawn him out
that day. While he was doing this, *Millefont* had time to examine his Face, thinking at firft, that he had feen him before,
tho' where, he could not prefently recollect ;
but the Tone of his Voice affifting the Idea
his Features had given him, he now remember'd this was one of thofe Gentlemen he
had feen at the Play-Houfe, and heard burft
out into fuch extravagant Encomiums on
the *Beggar's Opera*. It came prefently
into his Head to retort upon him in a merry
way ; which he did in thefe words. This,
Sir, *faid he*, is but the Sequel of the *Beggar's Opera* ; and I hope no Gentleman will
be offended at the *Reality*, who was de-
lighted with the *Reprefentation*. 'Tis, methinks, a charitable Confideration of the
Town, that fince the *South-Sea*, Bubbles, 11,12
and other publick Calamities have made fo
D 2   many

---

11. *South-Sea*: the great financial disaster in 1720 occasioned by the plunge in value
    of South Sea Company stock
12. Bubbles: delusive financial or commercial schemes' *O.E.D.*

many Beggars, this way of being fupply'd
by the Pockets of the more fortunate fhould
be encouraged. To take a Purfe by Violence or Stratagem from thofe not inclin'd
to beftow it, was, indeed, in former un-
fafhionable Times, thought fcandalous; and
not all the Bravery, nor Generofity of *Hind*,
————, or the *Golden Farmer*, could gain
them any better Titles than Rogue, and
Thief. But now, thanks to the *Beggar's
Opera*, 'tis become an agreeable and a lau-
dable Employment, engaging to the Men,
and charming to the Women; and a young
Fellow need not doubt but by it to raife his
Fortune from the one, and his Pleafures from
the other.

These Satirical Reflections, 'tis probable,
vex'd the Gentleman no lefs than the lofs
of his Money, but he made no anfwer,
neither liking the Remonftrance, nor the
Company of the Perfon who made it; and
therefore immediately held out his Purfe
and Watch. But our accomplifh'd Thief
would by no means accept the latter, telling him, that fince *Jonathan Wild* was un-
fortunately taken off, and none as yet had
thought fit to affume the Character of
Peachum, the *Macheaths* had no way to
vend thofe fort of Commodities with fafety,
and

and therefore dealt all in Specie. On which the Gentleman put it up, well enough pleased with this part of his Irony, tho' he was not with the other.

What pass'd afterwards between the Lovers, and whether they prosecuted the design on which they came to that Wood, or not, is not at all material to the History of *Millefont.* I shall therefore take my leave of them, and attend this unfortunate Gentleman till he came to a Cross-Road, where, meeting a Person well mounted and alone; he encounter'd him with the usual Form, *Stand, and deliver.* But this happen'd to be one who, having a great quantity of Gold about him, was not so easily to be prevail'd with to resign it. He presented his Pistol to *Millefont* at the same time he did his, and with more success; for while the other miss'd his Mark, he lodg'd a Bullet in the upper part of *Millefont's* left Arm, who, feeling himself wounded, and equally agitated by Revenge as Interest, was about to try the other Pistol, when the Servant of the Gentleman he attack'd, having stay'd behind on some occasion, came galloping towards them. *Millefont* now found it as vain as dangerous to engage with both, and clapping Spurs to his Horse, avoided their pursuit

with

with all the diligence he was Master of.
The many Cross-Roads he took, obliged
him to go so far out of his way, that it was
late before he reach'd *London*; where, being come to his Lodgings, a Surgeon was
sent for; he pretending he had got the
Wound by an Encounter with a Highwayman, who had attempted to rob him.
None suspected the Truth of what he said,
nor in the least imagin'd he had suffer'd his
Principles to be so far corrupted, as to have
got his Hurt by any means that were not
warrantable: And perhaps he might have
prosecuted the vile Profession he had taken
up, for a long time, without any body's sup-
posing him to be guilty of it, till grown
more bold and hardy in it, he had attack'd
some Persons as resolute as himself, and
been taken and brought to the Bar an Example of publick Justice. But Heaven, in
compassion to those virtuous Principles,
which had stood the Test of so many
Temptations, and at last yielded but to the
most poignant Necessity, was pleased to spare
that Shame, and take him off while high in
the good opinion of the World.

His Wound being searched, it was found
to be of such a nature, that the Surgeon de-
spair'd of making a Cure of him; and tho'
he

he did not in plain words tell him the worſt,
yet the Patient eaſily perceiv'd what his
Thoughts were, by his Looks, and the private Whiſpers he obſerved between him and
the Perſons preſent at the Operation: on
which he preſſingly deſired they would let
him know the certainty; adding, that if it
were true that he muſt die, he had much
to do before his departure; and to leave
any part of what he had to ſay undeclared,
would make him leave the World in Agonies ſuch as they would repent to have in-
flicted. Theſe Adjurations made the Sur- 13
geon, tho' unwillingly, let him know, that
there was ſcarce a probability of his Life;
but aſſured him, that he ſhould be a better
judge the next day, when he ſhould come
to open his Wound.

Millefont reſted ſatisfied with this Pro-
miſe, and waited the reſult; which happening, as he before imagin'd, a poſitive
Sentence of Death, he deſir'd a Clergyman
of the Church of *England* might be ſent
for, to whom he confeſs'd, in the preſence
of thoſe who attended him in his Illneſs,
the Crimes he had of late been guilty of,
and the Incitements he had to encourage him
to take up the Profeſſion of a Robber, con-
cluding with a hearty Prayer, that he might
be

---

13. Adjurations: solemn swearings

be the only Perſon ſeduced by the extravagant Applauſe the Town gave the Cha-
raƈter of a Thief in the *Beggar's Opera.*

He had ſcarce ended this declaration,
when his Siſter came into the Room, having
notice of his Hurt; but not appriz'd of the
Danger, imagin'd ſhe brought him news
which would go a great way toward the
haſtning his Recovery.   And before ſhe
could be told the truth of his Condition,
began to relate, how a Gentleman of above
fifteen hundred Pounds a Year, being dead
without any Heir, had left his whole Eſtate
to *Millefont,* who was of the ſame Name.

O Heaven! thou art juſt (*cry'd he*, as ſoon
as ſhe had finiſh'd her Narration :) How great
a Reward was preparing for me, had I per-
ſever'd in Innocence! but when I had re-
nounced thoſe Principles to which my Youth
was bred, how unfit was it I ſhould reap the
Benefit of thy gracious Decree!   How
wretched does he deſerve to be, who cannot truſt the Power that made him, for
Support!

Theſe Expreſſions throwing the young
Lady into the utmoſt Conſternation, ſhe was
by the Standers-by inform'd of all her Brother

ther had juft before reveal'd, together with the impoffibility he could out-live that Night. The Grief, which Tidings fo un-expected and alarming threw her into, may eafily be conceiv'd by what has been already faid of the tender Affection between them. I fhall therefore forbear troubling my Reader with any Repetition of what fhe faid, they being only fuch things as were natural to her Love and Virtue.

Millefont endeavoured to moderate her 'Affliction, conjur'd her always to preferve her Innocence; and, as an Atonement for his own Guilt, order'd that ftrict Enquiry fhould be made after the Perfons whom he had robb'd, and all he had taken reftored with double Intereft: And after allotting five hundred Pounds *per Annum* to be paid out of the Eftate lately left him, for charitable Ufes, divided the Remainder between his two Sifters. He liv'd not many Hours after he had fign'd his Teftament, which time he devoted wholly to Prayer and Meditation; mingling with Entreaties of Forgivenefs for his own Sins, the moft fervent Suppli-cations, that Heaven would be pleafed to reftore the *Britifh* Genius to fome degree of its former Vigour, and that no more un-happy *Millefonts* might be debauched from
E   their

their firſt Principles by the Encouragement
given to the depraved and vicious Characters which compoſe the *Beggar's Opera*.

How far his Devotions will ſucceed, is
yet uncertain; for the Town ſeems ſtill to
languiſh under the ſame Diſeaſe, and for
any thing that can be gather'd from the
Symptoms, will not ſoon be cured. We
are apt indeed to flatter ourſelves with ſome
little hope from the following Account;
viz. That ſome Gentlemen, fam'd for a
ſuperiority of Wit, to prove themſelves
ſuch, laid a conſiderable Wager, that whatever they undertook to eſpouſe, ſhould pleaſe
14 the World *nemine contradicente,* as long as
they ſhould countenance it by their preſence.
The Agreement was, that it ſhould be ſomething which had in it not the leaſt ſhadow
of intrinſick Merit. The *Beggar's Opera*
being at that time *à propos* on the ſtocks,
that was pitch'd on for the deciſion, and accordingly was by the Wagerers cry'd up
and extoll'd.

If this be faɛt, theſe Gentlemen have
certainly the double Pleaſure of winning
the Stake, and at the ſame time knowing
themſelves the Arbitrators and Judges of
Wit, even in a Cauſe where their Cenſure
                                        muſt

---

14. *nemine contradicente:* no one contradicting

muſt be againſt Wit. But I rather fear this is an Excuſe which ſome ingenious Lovers of their Country have invented, to ſcreen the reigning Folly of the Times, and make that paſs for a Deſign, which is in reality a Depravity of Nature, and a Deficiency of that Spirit which formerly encouraged the Muſes Growth, and the Promotion of Learning and of Virtue.

F I N I S.

[Jonathan Swift]. The Intelligencer . . . Printed at Dublin. London Reprinted, and sold by A. Moor in St. Paul's Church-yard, and the Booksellers of London and Westminster. 1729. Number Three, pp. 15-25, the complete text.

one Part of my Defign is anfwered. However, it cannot be unfeafonable to expofe
Malice, Avarice, Brutality, and Hypocrify,
wherever we find it.

NUMBER III.

————*Ipfe per omnes*
Ibit perfonas, & turbam reddet in unam. 1

THE *Players* having now almoft done
with the Comedy, called the *Beggars
Opera* for this Seafon, it may be no unplea-
fant Speculation, to reflect a little upon this
Dramatick Piece, fo fingular in the Subject,
and the Manner fo much an Original, and
which hath frequently given fo very agreeable an Entertainment.

ALTHOUGH an evil *Tafte* be very apt
to prevail, both here and in *London*, yet
there is a Point, which whoever can rightly
touch, will never fail of pleafing a very
great Majority; fo great, that the Diflikers,
out of Dulnefs or Affectation will be filent,
and

---

1. *unam*: he will go through all the characters and make them into one group.

and forced to fall in with the Herd: The Point I mean, is what we call *Humour*, which in its Perfection is allowed to be much preferable to *Wit*, if it be not rather the moft ufeful, and agreeable Species of it.

2   I agree with Sir *William Temple*, that the Word is peculiar to our *English Tongue*; but I differ from him in the Opinion, that the

3   Thing it felf is peculiar to the *English Nation*, becaufe the contrary may be found in many *Spanish*, *Italian* and *French* Productions, and particularly, whoever hath a *Tafte* for *True Humour*, will find a hundred Inftances of it in thofe Volumes printed in

4   *France*, under the Name of *Le Theatre Italien*, to fay nothing of *Rabelais*, *Cervantes*, and many others.

Now I take the *Comedy* or *Farce*, (or whatever Name the *Criticks* will allow it) called the *Beggars Opera*, to excel in this Article of *Humour*, and upon that Merit to have met with fuch prodigious Succefs both here and in *England*.

As to *Poetry*, *Eloquence* and *Mufick*, which are faid to have moft Power over the Minds

3   of

2. Sir *William Temple:* 1628-99, statesman and essayist, patron of Swift
3. *Nation:* in *Of Poetry* (*Critical Essays of the Seventeeth Century*, ed. J. E. Spingarn, III, 103-4.)
4. *Italien: Le Théâtre Italien, ou le Receuil de toutes les Comédies et Scènes Fran-çoises, qui ont été jouées sur le Théâtre Italien,* ed. Evariste Ghérardi, a collection begun in 1695.

of Men, it is certain that very few have a
Taſte or *Judgment* of the Excellencies of the
two former; and if a Man ſucceeds in either,
it is upon the Authority of thoſe *few Judges*,
that lend their *Taſte* to the Bulk of Readers,
who have none of their own. I am told
there are as few good Judges in *Muſick*, and
that among thoſe who crowd the *Opera's*,
Nine in Ten go thither merely out of *Curi-
oſity, Faſhion*, or *Affectation*.

BUT a *Taſte* for *Humour* is in ſome Manner fixed to the very Nature of Man, and
generally obvious to the Vulgar, except upon Subjects too refined, and ſuperior to their
Underſtanding.

AND as this *Taſte* of *Humour* is purely
Natural, ſo is *Humour* it ſelf, neither is it a
Talent confined to Men of *Wit*, or *Learning*; for we obſerve it ſometimes among common Servants, and the Meaneſt of the People, while the very Owners are often ignorant of the Gift they poſſeſs.

I KNOW very well, that this happy *Talent*
is contemptibly treated by *Criticks*, under
the Name of *low Humour*, or *low Comedy*;

C   but

but I know likewise, that the *Spaniards* and *Italians*, who are allowed to have the moſt Wit of any *Nation* in *Europe*, do moſt excel in it, and do moſt eſteem it.

BY what Diſpoſition of the Mind, what Influence of the Stars, or what Situation of the *Climate* this Endowment is beſtowed upon Mankind, may be a Queſtion fit for *Philoſophers* to diſcuſs. It is certainly the beſt Ingredient towards that Kind of Satyr, which is moſt uſeful, and gives the leaſt Offence; which inſtead of laſhing, laughs Men out of their Follies, and Vices, and is the Character which gives *Horace* the Preference to *Juvenal*.

AND although ſome Things are too ſerious, ſolemn, or ſacred to be turned into Ridicule, yet the Abuſes of them are certainly not, ſince it is allowed that Corruption in *Religion*, *Politicks*, and *Law*, may be proper *Topicks* for this Kind of *Satyr*.

THERE are two Ends that Men propoſe in writing Satyr, one of them leſs Noble than the other, as regarding nothing further than perſonal Satisfaction, and Pleaſure of the
Writer;

Writer, but without any View towards *Per-*
fonal Malice; the other is a *Publick Spirit*,
prompting Men of *Genius* and Virtue, to
mend the World as far as they are able
And as both these Ends are innocent, so the
latter is highly commendable. With Regard to the former, I demand whether I have
not as good a Title to laugh, as Men have to
be ridiculous, and to expose Vice, as another
hath to be vicious. If I ridicule the Follies
and Corruptions of a *Court*, a *Miniftry*, or
a *Senate*, are they not amply paid by *Penfi-*
ons, *Titles*, and *Power*, while I expect and
defire no other Reward, than that of laughing with a few Friends in a Corner? Yet,
if those who take Offence, think me in the
Wrong, I am ready to change the Scene
with them, whenever they please.

BUT if my Defign be to make Mankind
better, then I think it is my Duty; at least
I am sure it is the Intereft of thofe very
Courts and *Minifters*, whofe Follies or Vices
I ridicule, to reward me for my good Inten-
tions: For if it be reckoned a high Point of
Wifdom to get the Laughers on our Side, it

C 2   is

is much more Eafy, as well as Wife to get thofe on our Side, who can make Millions laugh when they pleafe.

MY Reafon for mentioning *Courts*, and *Miniſters*, (whom I never think on but with the moſt profound Veneration) is, becaufe an Opinion obtains that in the *Beggars Opera* there appears to be fome Reflection upon *Courtiers* and *Stateſmen*, whereof I am by no Means a Judge.

IT is true indeed, that Mr. GAY, the Author of this Piece, hath been fomewhat fingular in the Courfe of his Fortunes; for it hath happened, that after Fourteen Years attending the *Court*, with a large Stock of real Merit, a modeſt and agreeable Converfation, a *Hundred Promiſes* and *Five Hundred Friends*, hath failed of Preferment, and upon a very weighty Reafon. He lay under the Sufpicion of having written a Libel, or Lampoon againſt a great M-------. It is true that great M------ was demonſtratively convinced, and publickly owned his Conviction, that Mr. GAY was not the Author; but having lain under the Sufpicion, it

---

5. or Lampoon: Walpole believed Gay to be the author of a lampoon against himself and had reported on Gay unfavorably to the Queen
6. M_: Minister, Sir Robert Walpole

it feemed very juft, that he fhould fuffer the Punifhment; becaufe in this moft reformed Age, the Virtues of a great M----- are no more to be fufpected, than the Chaftity of *Cæfar's* Wife.

IT muft be allowed, That the *Beggars Opera* is not the firft of Mr. GAY's Works, wherein he hath been faulty, with Regard to *Courtiers* and *Statefmen.* For to omit his other Pieces, even in his Fables, publifhed within two Years paft, and dedicated to the *Duke of* CUMBERLAND, for which 7 he was PROMISED a Reward, he hath been thought fomewhat too bold upon *Courtiers.* And although it is highly probable, he meant only the *Courtiers* of former Times, yet he acted unwarily, by not confidering that the Malignity of fome People might mifinterpret what he faid to the Difadvantage of prefent *Perfons* and Affairs.

BUT I have now done with Mr. GAY as a Politician, and fhall confider him henceforward only as Author of the *Beggars Opera*, wherein he hath by a Turn of *Humour*, entirely New, placed Vices of all Kinds in the

C 3   ftrongeft

---

7. Cumberland: William Augustus, 3rd Duke of Cumberland, 2nd son of George, Prince of Wales, for whom Gay wrote his *Fables*

ftrongeft and moft odious Light; and thereby done eminent Service, both to *Religion*
and *Morality*.   This appears from the unpa-
rallell'd Succefs he hath met with. All *Ranks*,
Parties and *Denominations* of Men either
crowding to fee his *Opera*, or reading it with
Delight in their Clofets, even *Minifters* of
State, whom he is thought to have moft offended (next to thofe whom the Actors more
immediately reprefent) appearing frequently
at the *Theatre*, from a Confcioufnefs of their
own Innocence, and to convince the World
how unjuft a Parallel, *Malice, Envy* and
Difaffection to the Government have made.

    I AM affured that feveral worthy *Clergy-*
Men in this *City*, went privately to fee the
Beggars Opera reprefented; and that the
fleering Coxcombs in the *Pit*, amufed themfelves with making Difcoveries, and fpread-
ing the Names of thofe Gentlemen round the
Audience.

    I SHALL not pretend to vindicate a *Clergy-*
man, who would appear openly in his Habit at a *Theatre*, among fuch a vicious Crew,
as would probably ftand round him, and at
                                                    fuch

such lewd *Comedies,* and prophane *Tragedies* as are often reprefented. Befides I know very well, that Perfons of their Function are bound to avoid the Appearance of Evil, or of giving Caufe of Offence. But when the *Lords Chancellors,* who are Keepers of the King's Confcience; when the *Judges* of the Land, whofe Title is *Reverend*; when *Ladies,* who are bound by the Rules of their Sex to the ftricteft Decency, appear in the *Theatre* without Cenfure, I cannot underftand, why a young Clergy-man who goes concealed out of Curiofity to fee an innocent and moral Play, fhould be fo highly condemned; nor do I much approve the Rigour of a great P----te, who faid, *he hoped none of his Clergy were there.* I am glad to hear there are 8 no weightier Objections againft that Reverend Body, planted in this City, and I wifh there never may. But I fhould be very forry that any of them fhould be fo weak, as to imitate a COURT-CHAPLAIN in *England,* 9 who preached againft the *Beggars Opera,* which will probably do more Good than a thoufand Sermons of fo ftupid, fo injudicious, and fo proftitute a Divine.   C 4   IN

---

8. P_te: Prelate
9. Court-Chaplain: Dr. Thomas Herring; see introduction to this chapter

IN this happy Performance of Mr. GAY's,
all the Characters are juſt, and none of them
carried beyond Nature, or hardly beyond
Practice.   It diſcovers the whole Syſtem of
that Common-Wealth, or that *Imperium in
Imperio* of Iniquity, eſtabliſhed among us,
by which neither our Lives, nor our Properties are ſecure, either in the High-ways, or in
publick Aſſemblies, or even in our own Houſes.   It ſhews the miſerable Lives and the
conſtant Fate of thoſe abandoned Wretches;
for how little they ſell their Lives and Souls;
betrayed by their *Whores,* their *Comrades,*
and the *Receivers* and *Purchaſers* of theſe
Thefts and Robberies.   This *Comedy* contains likewiſe a *Satyr,* which although it
doth by no Means affect the preſent Age, yet
might have been uſeful in the former, and
may poſſibly be ſo in Ages to come: I mean
where the Author takes Occaſion of comparing thoſe *common Robbers of the Publick,*
and their ſeveral Stratagems of betraying, un-
dermining and hanging each other, to the
ſeveral Arts of *Politicians* in Times of Corruption.

THIS

---

10. *Imperium in Imperio*: kingdom within a kingdom

THIS *Comedy* likewise expoſeth with great Juſtice that unnatural Taſte for *Italian* Muſick among us, which is wholly unſuitable to our Northern *Climate*, and the *Genius* of the People, whereby we are overrun with *Italian-Effeminacy*, and *Italian* Nonſenſe. An old Gentleman ſaid to me, that many Years ago, when the Practice of an unnatural Vice grew ſo frequent in *London* that many were proſecuted for it, he was ſure it would be the Fore-runner of *Italian Opera's* and Singers; and then we ſhould want nothing but ſtabbing or poyſoning, to make us perfect *Italians*.

UPON the Whole, I deliver my Judgment, That nothing but ſervile Attachment to a Party, Affectation of Singularity, lamentable Dullneſs, miſtaken Zeal, or ſtudied Hypocriſy, can have the leaſt reaſonable Objection againſt this excellent moral Performance of the CELEBRATED MR. GAY.

Boswell, whose response to *The Beggar's Opera* is usually oversimplified by critics, managed both to admit the immorality of the play and to admire the Opera enormously. He felt Johnson underestimated the appeal to a youthful imagination of the gaiety and heroism of highwaymen and of their easy method of acquiring private property. Boswell was, of course, talking about himself. The figure of Macheath, Frederick Pottle has noted,[1] in one way or another dominates the *London Journal*, as the following seraglio incident suggests:

> We [Boswell and two very pretty girls] were shown into a good room and had a bottle of sherry before us in a minute. I surveyed my seraglio and found them both good subjects for amorous play. I toyed with them and drank about and sung *Youth's the Season* [Air XXII] and thought myself Captain Macheath; and then I solaced my existence with them, one after the other, according to their seniority.[2]

1. *Boswell's London Journal*, ed. Frederick Pottle (New York: Mc Graw-Hill, 1950), p. 252, n.7.
2. *Boswell's London Journal*, p. 264.

Boswell's Life of Johnson, ed. George Birkbeck Hill, revised by L. F. Powell (Oxford: Clarendon Press, 1934), II, 367-368

'The Beggar's Opera,' and the common question, whether it was pernicious in its effects, having been introduced;—Johnson. 'as to this matter, which has been very much contested, I myself am of opinion, that more influence has been ascribed to "The Beggar's Opera," than it in reality ever had: for I do not believe that any man was ever made a rogue by being present at its representation. At the same time I do not deny that it may have some influence, by making the character of a rogue familiar, and in some degree pleasing.' Then collecting himself, as it were, to give a heavy stroke: 'There is in it such a *labefactation*[1] of all principles, as may be injurious to morality.'

While he pronounced this response, we sat in a comical sort of restraint, smothering a laugh, which we were afraid might burst out. In his Life of Gay, he has been still more decisive as to the inefficiency of 'The Beggar's Opera' in corrupting society. But I have ever thought some what differently; for, indeed, not only are the gaiety and heroism of a highwayman very captivating to a youthful imagination, but the arguments for adventurous depredation are so plausible, the allusions so lively, and the contrasts with the ordinary and more painful modes of acquiring property are so artfully displayed, that it requires a cool and strong judgement to resist so imposing an aggregate: yet, I own, I should be very sorry to have 'The Beggar's Opera' suppressed; for there is in it so much of real London life, so much brilliant wit, and such a variety of airs, which, from early association of ideas, engage, soothe, and enliven the mind, that no performance which the theatre exhibits, delights me more.

1. weakening; overthrow

VI. The First Season

The first night of *The Beggar's Opera*, 29 January 1728, is one of the great moments in the history of the eighteenth century theatre. The following accounts from Pope's letters, a newspaper, Spence, Boswell, and early histories of the theatre convey vividly the anxiety of Gay and his friends whether his very odd piece would "take," and the unnervingly delayed reactions of the audience. It must be remembered that audiences were sometimes so violent in expressing their disapproval that the performance could not continue.

The Correspondence of Alexander Pope, ed. George Sherburn (Oxford: Clarendon Press, 1956), Pope to Swift, January 1728, II, 469.

John Gay's Opera is just on the point of Delivery. It may be call'd (considering its Subject) a Jayl-Delivery. Mr. Congreve (with whom I have commemorated you) is anxious as to its Success, and so am I; whether it succeeds or not, it will make a great noise, but whether of Claps or Hisses I know not. At worst it is in its own nature a thing which he can *lose* no reputation by, as he lays none upon it.

The Daily Journal, February 1, 1728

On Monday was represented for the first Time, at the Theatre Royal in Lincoln's Inn Fields, Mr. Gay's new English Opera, written in a Manner wholly new, and very entertaining, there being introduced, instead of Italian Airs, about 60 of the most celebrated old English and Scotch Tunes. There was present, then, as well as last Night, a prodigious Concourse of Nobility and Gentry, and no Theatrical Performance for these many Years has met with so much Applause.

William Oxberry, *Dramatic Biography*, 5 vols. London, 1825-26. IV, 177.

The first night the *Beggar's Opera* was played at the Lincoln's-inn-fields theatre, the audience, not being then much acquainted with the nature of operas, expected the usual music before the drawing up of the curtain—finding themselves (as they imagined) likely to be bilked out of their first and second music,[1] they expressed great disapprobation, insomuch that Jack Hall (the original Lockit) was sent on to apologise for the omission, by explaining that it was a rule to have no music prior to the overture. Jack made his obeisance with a tolerable grace, but being confounded at the general silence which so suddenly ensued on his appearance, blundered out —"Ladies and gentlemen, we—we—beg you'll not call for first and second music, because—because you all know, that there is never any music at all in an opera." This bull[2] put the house in good humour, and the piece proceeded.

---

1. instrumental music before the beginning of the play
2. 'an expression involving a ludicrous inconsistency' *O.E.D.*

Joseph Spence, *Observations, Anecdotes, and Characters of Books and Men,* ed. James M. Osborn (Oxford: Clarendon Press, 1966), I, 106-7.

(Spence here records the words of his friend Pope.)

We were all at the first night of it [*The Beggar's Opera*] in great uncertainty of the event, till we were very much encouraged by overhearing the Duke of Argyle,[1] who sat in the next box to us, say, 'It will do—it must do! I see it in the eyes of them.' This was a good while before the first act was over, and so gave us ease soon, for that Duke, besides his own good taste, has as particular a knack as any one now living in discovering the taste of the public. He was quite right in this, as usual. The good nature of the audience appeared stronger and stronger every act, and ended in a clamor of applause.

---

1. John Campbell (1678-1743) second Duke of Argyle, opponent of Sir Robert Walpole

Boswell's Life of Johnson, II, 368-9.

The late *'worthy'* Duke of Queensbury[1] . . . told me, that when Gay first shewed him 'The Beggar's Opera,' his Grace's observation was, 'This is a very odd thing, Gay; I am satisfied that it is either a very good thing, or a very bad thing.' It proved the former, beyond the warmest expectations of the author or his friends. Mr. Cambridge,[2] however, shewed us to day, that there was good reason enough to doubt concerning its success. He was told by Quin, that during the first night of its appearance it was long in a very dubious state; that there was a disposition to damn it, and that it was saved by the song [Air XII]

'Oh ponder well! be not severe!'

the audience being much affected by the innocent looks of Polly, when she came to those two lines, which exhibit at once a painful and ridiculous image,

'For on the rope that hangs my Dear,
Depends poor Polly's life.'

---

1. Charles Douglas, third Duke of Queensbury and his wife, Catherine Hyde, were close friends and ardent supporters of Gay, with whom he spent most of the last four years of his life.
2. Richard Owen Cambridge, minor poet and friend of Boswell's.

Quin himself had so bad an opinion of it, that he refused the part of Captain Macheath, and gave it to Walker, who acquired great celebrity by his grave yet animated performance of it.[3]

Benjamin Victor, *The History Of The Theatres Of London and Dublin* . . . London, 1761, II, 154.

. . . on the first Night of Performance, its Fate was doubtful for some Time. The first Act was received with silent Attention, not a Hand moved; at the End of which they rose, and every Man seemed to compare Notes with his Neighbour, and the general Opinion was in its Favour. In the second Act they broke their Silence, by Marks of their Approbation, to the great Joy of the frightened Performers, as well as the Author; and the last Act was received with universal Applause.

---

3. See p. 165.

Pope's often quoted note in *The Dunciad* is the best succinct account of the *Opera's* enormous vogue. We give what is apparently the first appearance in print of the famous punning *bon mot*, some newspaper advertisements that illustrate Pope's note, and excerpts from the Pope-Swift-Gay correspondence that show delight at Gay's success and his profits.

Alexander Pope, *The Dunciad*, ed. James Sutherland (London: Methuen, 1963), (A) III, 326,n.

The vast success of it [*The Beggar's Opera*] was unprecedented, and almost incredible: What is related of the wonderful effects of the ancient Music or Tragedy hardly came up to it: *Sophocles* and *Euripides* were less follow'd and famous. It was acted in *London* sixty-three days, uninterrupted; and renew'd the next season with equal applauses. It spread into all the great towns of *England*, was play'd in many places to the 30th, and 40th time, at *Bath* and *Bristol* 50, &c. It made its progress into *Wales, Scotland,* and *Ireland,* where it was performed 24 days together. It was lastly acted in *Minorca.* The fame of it was not confin'd to the author only; the Ladies carry'd about with 'em the favourite songs of it in Fans; and houses were furnish'd with it in Screens. The person who acted *Polly,* till then obscure, became all at once the favourite of the town; her *Pictures* were ingraved and sold in great numbers; her *Life* written; books of *Letters* and *Verses* to her publish'd; and pamphlets made even of her *Sayings* and *Jests.*

Furthermore, it drove out of *England* the *Italian Opera* which had carry'd all before it for ten years: That Idol of the Nobility and the people, which the great Critick Mr. *Dennis*[1] by the labours and outcries of a whole life could not overthrow, was demolish'd in one winter by a single stroke of this gentleman's pen. This remarkable period happen'd in the year 1728. Yet so great was his modesty, that he constantly prefixed to all the editions of it this Motto, *Nos haec novimus esse nihil.*[2]

---

1. John Dennis, critic and enemy of Pope, well-known for his dislike of Italian opera.
2. Martial's *Epigrams*, XIII, ii, 8. Literally: we know these things to be nothing.

The Craftsman, 3 February 1728.

This week a Dramatick Entertainment has been exhibited at the Theatre in Lincoln's-Inn Fields, entitled *the Beggar's Opera*, which has met with a general Applause, insomuch that the Waggs say it has made *Rich*[1] very *Gay*, and probably will make *Gay* very *Rich*.

The Craftsman, 18 May 1728.

The Publick hath been lately imposed on in so many senseless and insipid Pamphlets, especially with Relation to the *Beggar's Opera*, that Gentlemen are justly discouraged from buying any, till they receive a particular Character of them. For this Reason I am induced to recommend a little Piece just published, intitled *Some Memoirs of the Life and Manners of Capt. Mackheath*, in which I will venture to promise my Readers a very agreeable Entertainment.

The Craftsman, 29 June 1728.

This Day is publish'd, and ready to be delivered to the Subscribers, The Beggar's Opera Screen; on which is curiously engrav'd on Copper-plates, the principal Captives of the All-conquering Polly, plainly describ'd by Hieroglyphicks; and on the Reverse their Amorous Letters and Declarations to that celebrated Warbler of Ribaldry. Design'd for the Instruction of the Curious and Inquisitive of both Sexes. The whole illustrated and adorn'd in their proper natural Colours, with Motto's suitable to their Quality. Printed for the Inventor, and sold at the Fan-shop next door to White's Chocolate-house in St. James's Street, and at Mrs. Vuljohn's a Milliner, at the Golden Leg in Cranbourn-Alley. Price 2s 6d.

The Craftsman, 29 June 1728.

Whereas the Town having been imposed on by Pamphlets publish'd in the Name of POLLY PEACHUM; this is to inform the Publick, that I never knew of any Pampelet made publick, save my Opera and Life, which were wrote by a Person that perform'd in the Beggar's Opera; and in Justice to the Author and myself, am oblig'ed to make this Publication, in hopes to put an End to all Scandal rais'd by those who are unacquainted with the Life and Character of POLLY PEACHUM.

P. S. Both which Pamphlets are to be had at all Pamphlet-Shops in London and Westminster, and hope those who buy my Life will judge without Partiality.

---

1. John Rich, mamager of the Theatre Royal, Lincoln's inn Fields where *The Beggar's Opera* was first performed

The Letters of John Gay, edited by C. F. Burgess. Oxford: Clarendon Press, 1966. Gay to Swift, 15 February 1728, pp. 70-71.

I have deferr'd writing to you from time to time till I could give you an account of the Beggar's Opera. It is Acted at the Playhouse in Lincoln's Inn fields, with such success that the Playhouse hath been crouded every night; to night is the fifteenth time of Acting, and 'tis thought it will run a fortnight longer. I have order'd Motte[1] to send the Play to you the first opportunity. I made no interest either for approbation or money nor hath any body been prest to take tickets for my Benefit,[2] notwithstanding which, I think I shall make an addition to my fortune of between six and seven hundred pounds. I know this account will give you pleasure, as I have push'd through this precarious Affair without servility or flattery. As to any favours from Great men I am in the same state you left me; but I am a great deal happier as I have no expectations. The Dutchess of Queensbury[3] hath signaliz'd her friendship to me upon this occasion in such a conspicuous manner, that I hope (for her sake) you will take care to put your fork to all its proper uses, and suffer nobody for the f[uture] to put their knives in their mouths. Lord Cobham[4] says that I should [have] printed it in Italian over against the English, that the Ladys might have understood what they read. The outlandish (as they now call it) Opera[5] hath been so thin of late that some have call'd that the Beggars Opera & if the run continues, I fear I shall have remonstrances drawn up agaist me by the Royal Academy of Musick.[6]

---

1. Benjamin Motte, bookseller and publisher for both Pope and Swift
2. a performance from which Gay would receive the proceeds
3. Catherine Hyde, Duchess of Queensbury, close friend and ardent supporter of Gay
4. Sir Richard Temple, Viscount Cobham, soldier, friend of Pope, and creator of the famous landscape gardens at Stowe
5. the Italian opera
6. which sponsored the Italian opera

The Letters of John Gay, Gay to Swift, 20 March 1728, pp. 72-73

The Beggar's Opera hath now been acted thirty-six times, and was as full the last night as the first, and as yet there is not the least probability of a thin audience; though there is a discourse about the town that the Directors of the Royal Academy of Musick[1] design to sollicite against its being play'd on the *outlandish* Opera days,[2] as it is now call'd. On the Benefit day[3] of one of the Actresse's last week one of the players falling sick they were oblig'd to give out another play or dismiss the Audience, A Play was given out, but people call'd for the Beggar's Opera, & they were forc'd to play it, or the Audience would not have stayd. I have got by all this success between seven & eight hundred pounds, and Rich[4] (deducting the whole charge of the House) hath clear'd already near four thousand pounds. . . . There is a Mezzo-tinto[5] Print publish'd to day of Polly, the Heroine of the Beggar's Opera, who was before unknown, & is now in so high vogue, that I am in doubt, whether her fame does not surpass that of the Opera itself.

The Correspondence of Alexander Pope, Pope to Swift, 23 March 1728. II,480.

Mr. Gay's Opera has acted near forty days running, and will certainly continue to the whole season. So he has more than a fence about his thousand pounds: he'll soon be thinking of a fence about his two thousand.

---

1. which sponsored the Italian opera
2. see the preceding letter
3. on which she would receive the proceeds
4. John Rich, manager of the Theatre Royal, Lincoln's inn Fields where *The Beggar's Opera* was first performed
5. a print made from a metal plate reproducing continuous tones of grey. The print was by John Faber the Younger (1695?-1756), after a painting by John Ellys or Ellis (1701-1757), who also painted Walker as Macheath.

The Correspondence of Alexander Pope, Swift to Gay, 28 March 1728, II, 482, 484.

We have your Opera for 6d[1] and we are as full of it pro modulo nostro[2] as London can be continuall acting, and house Crammd, and the Lord Lieut [3] severall times there, laughing his heart out I wish you had sent me a Copy as I desired to oblige an honest Bookseller, it would have done Motte[4] no hurt, for no English copy has been sold out but the Dublin one has run prodigiously. I did not understand that the Scene of Locket and Peachum's quarrels[5] was an imitation of one between Brutus and Cassius[6] till I was told it; I wish Mackheath when he was going to be hang'd had imitated Alexdr the great when he was dying. I would have had his fellow rogues, desire his commands about a Successor, and he to answer, let it be the most worthy: &c, we hear a million of Story's about the opera, of the ancore at the Song, *That was levelled at me,*[7] when 2 Great Ministers[8] were in a Box together, and all the world staring at them I am heartily glad your opera hath mended your purse though perhaps it may Spoyl your Court I think that rich rogue Rich[9] Should in conscience make you a present of 2 or 3 hundred Guineas.[10] I am impatient that Such a dog by Sitting Still Should get five times more than the Author. you told me a month ago of 700 11, and have you not quite made up the Eight yet, I know not your methods. how many third days[11] are you allowd, and how much is each day worth, and what did you get for the Copy? . . . The Beggers Opera hath knockt down Gulliver, I hope to see Popes Dullness[12] knock down the Beggers Opera, but not till it hath fully done its Jobb.

---

1. the price, apparently, of the Dublin edition
2. by our standard
3. John Lord Carteret, Lord Lieutenant of Ireland
4. Benjamin Motte, bookseller and publisher for both Pope and Swift
5. II,x
6. *Julius Caesar*, IV,iii
7. Air XXX
8. the reference is apparently to Sir Robert Walpole and an unidentified friend. See the excerpt from Cooke's *Memoirs of Charles Macklin* in 'The Political Background.'
9. John Rich, manager of the Theatre Royal, Lincoln's Inn Fields where *The Beggar's Opera* was first performed
10. the guinea was an English coin worth 21 shillings
11. benefit days, when Gay would receive the proceeds
12. *The Dunciad*, published 18 May 1728. *Gulliver's Travels* had been published in 1726; *The Beggar's Opera* was first performed on 29 January 1728 and first published on 14 February.

Gay and Rich were not the only ones to profit handsomely from the *Opera*; Lavinia Fenton in the role of Polly became a star overnight. The natural daughter of a Mr. Beswick, a lieutenant in the Royal Navy, and Mrs. Fenton, a keeper of a coffeehouse in Charing Cross, she had her debut in *The Orphan* at the Haymarket theatre in March, 1726. Before 1728 she had played Cherry in *The Beaux' Stratagem* and Monimia in *Venice Preserv'd*. Her great conquest was Charles Powlett, Duke of Bolton, who became so enchanted with her as she sang "Oh, ponder well" that he returned night after night to watch her perform. At the end of the first season she left the cast to become his mistress. Twenty-three years later, on the death of the Duchess of Bolton, he married her. There was another side to her vogue, of course: Edward Young is unkind: "She, 'tis said, has raised her Price from one Guinea to a 100, tho she cannot be a greater whore than she was before, nor, I suppose, a younger."[1] We print three out of the many (mostly very bad) poems she inspired which reflect her dubious brief fame.

Thomas Walker, the original Macheath, made less of a stir than Polly but remains the most famous of Macheaths. Rich had originally intended to use James Quin, one of the best known actors of the day, but Quin seems to have had little desire to play a highwayman and little confidence in his singing ability. Tom Walker, so the story goes, was heard humming the tunes backstage, "in a tone and liveliness of manner" which attracted the notice of the cast. Quin laid hold of this circumstance to get rid of the part, and exclaimed, "Aye, there's a man who is much more qualified to do you justice than I am." Walker was called on to make the experiment; and Gay, who instantly saw the difference, accepted him as the hero of his piece" (Cooke, *Memoirs of Charles Macklin*, pp. 27-28). With, apparently, little formal training in acting or singing, he made a handsome romantic hero. He died of drink, in poverty, in Dublin when he was only forty-six.

---

1. Richard Eustace Tickell, *Thomas Tickell and the Eighteenth Century Poets* (London: Constable, 1931), p. 145.

A NEW
BALLAD,

Infcrib'd to

POLLY PEACHUM.

To the Tune of *Pretty Parrot fay.*

I.

P RETTY *Polly* fay,
1   When did *Jo—y G—y*
2 *St—ch* you, *St—ch* you, for his Play,
     In which you 'pear fo charming;
     Does he *St—ch,*
     With a Twitch,
3   As well as *R—h,*
4 Or does he *S—e* you ftorming;
     Whilft you do fondly loll,
     Whilft you do fondly loll,
     O pretty, pretty *Poll.*

II. Tell

"A New Ballad, Inscrib'd to Polly Peachum," in The Twickenham Hotch-Potch For the Use of the Rev. Dr. Swift, Alexander Pope, Esq; and Company. Being A Sequel To The Beggars Opera . . . London: Printed for J. Roberts in Warwick-Lane. 1728. Pp. 10-17.

---

1. *Je_y G_y*: Johnny Gay
2. *St_ch*: stitch, copulate
3. *R_ch*: Rich; John Rich, manager of the Theatre Royal, Lincoln Inn Fields, where
     The Beggar's Opera was first produced
4. *S_e*: swive, copulate

166

II.

Tell us how he plays,
　How his Fingers ſtrays;
Tell us all his various Ways,
　How he his Shot diſcharges:
　　Is his Veins
　　Like his Brains,
　　When in Strains,
He a Theme enlarges?
　Sure 'tis a pleaſant Droll,
　Sure 'tis a pleaſant Droll,
　O pretty, pretty *Poll.*

III.

But not only he,
　Men of high Degree
Are as fond, as fond of Thee,
　As the *German* Count thy Keeper;
　　For a T—ſt,
　　Gold like Duſt,
　　But unjuſt,
Thou didſt play the Sweeper;
　And thou didſt with others fall,
　And thou didſt with others fall,
　O wicked, wicked *Poll.*

D 2　　　　　　　　IV. Old

IV.

Old Sir *R— F—g,*
With his jaded Nag,
Of a fwifter Art did brag,
   To run a Race with Vigour;
     But the Job,
     Made Sir *Bob*
     Sigh and Sob,
This was *Venus* Rigour:
   For you did his Courage pall,
   For you did his Courage pall,
   O pretty, pretty *Poll.*

V.

No *New-Market* Race,
Brought him fuch Difgrace,
He was diftanc'd in the Chace,
   And from his Steed difmounted:
     He'll no more brag,
     Of his Nag,
     He does flag,
And *run* as it's recounted:
   Thus, thou doft ferve 'em all,
   Thus, thou doft ferve 'em all,
   O pretty, pretty *Poll.*

VI. B—d's

VI.

B—d's pretty *D—e*,
Wounded by a Look,
Would come in too for a Stroke,
 And from the Stage he had thee:
  O sweet Joy,
  Noble Boy,
  Pretty Toy,
He will not upbraid thee;
 Tho' others on thee Fall,
 Tho' others on thee Fall,
 O pretty, pretty *Poll.*

VII.

L—d T—y came,
Full of Fire and Flame,
Panting, panting for the Game,
 Like a Youth in Flower:
  To gain his Ends
  How he spends,
  And descends
In a Golden Shower:
 Such may have thee at their Call,
 Such may have thee at their Call,
 O pretty, pretty *Poll.*

      VIII. Then

VIII.

Then came Sir *J—n H—l*,
Thund'ring at thy Cupboard ;
But you caſt him like a Lubbard,
And did ſoon diſpatch him :
  For the Knight
  Spit his Spite,
  And tir'd quite,
Since thou didſt o'er Match him :
  For thou didſt his Vigour maul,
  For thou didſt his Vigour maul,
  O pretty, nimble *Poll*.

IX.

S—e, tho' in State,
Is both Good and Great ;
Yet he put in for the Plate,
  Running at a Venture :
  Was his Trick
  Politick,
  Did his
Meet you in the Centre :
  Tho' he flew, thou mad'ſt him crawl,
  Tho' he flew, thou mad'ſt him crawl,
  O pretty, pretty *Poll*.

X. Thus

X.

Thus the Stars we fee,
Lend their Light to thee;
Bright and Glorious thou muft be,
Who art fo much fhin'd on:
Happy Days,
If thy Rays
Do not Blaze,
So as to Fire and Blind one;
Then thou wilt loudly bawl,
Then thou wilt loudly bawl,
O poor unhappy *Poll.*

XI.

O thou pretty Toaft,
Fops with Joy do boaft
That with Eafe they rule the Roaft,
And thou'rt always ready;
But I fay,
Make them pay
For their Play;
If thou't be a Lady,
Learn to rife as well as fall,
Learn to rife as well as fall,
O pretty, pretty *Poll.*

XII. There-

XII.

Therefore pretty *Poll*,
Give each Fop a Fall;
Never, never End the Droll
   Without Coach and Horses:
      You're in Prime,
      Ufe your Time,
      What is S——
Cupid has his Croffes:
   And he will wound thy Gall,
   And he will wound thy Gall,
   O pretty, pretty *Poll.*

XIII.

If a Conflagration
Makes a Perturbation,
There is Smarting and Vexation,
   Guineas fly for *Bolus*;
      Then the Quire
      Do retire,
      Fearing *Fire,*
And they leave you *Solus:*
   Then take heed how you fall,
   Then take heed how you fall,
   O pretty, pretty *Poll.*

XIV. Yet,

XIV.

Yet, dear *Poll*, you may
Suffer *J—y G—y*
For to *S—h* you for his Play,
  Which has rais'd your Grandeur;
    Before which
    You would *S—h*
    Near *Fleet-Ditch*,
P—le was your Pindar:
  Then don't you vaunt it over all,
  Then don't you vaunt it over all,
  Tho' you are pretty *Poll*.

A NEW
BALLAD.
BY
CALEB D'ANVERS.

To the Tune of, *Sally in our Alley*

I.

O F all the Belles that tread the Stage,
    There's none like pretty *Polly*,
And all the Mufick of the Age,
    Except her Voice, is Folly;
1 The waining Nymphs of *Drury-Lane*
    I now can bear no longer;
And when fhe's prefent, I difdain
2,3   My *quondam* Favourite *Y-n--ger*.

II. Com-

"A New Ballad. By Caleb D'Anvers," in The Twickenham Hotch-Potch.
Pp. 38-40.

---

1. *Drury-Lane*: famous for its prostitutes
2. *quondam*: former
3. *Y_ger*: Elizabeth Younger, 1699?-1762, actress

174

II.

Compar'd with her, how flat appears
   Cuzzoni or *Fauſtina?*   4
And when ſhe ſings, I ſhut my Ears
   To warbling *Seneſino.*   5
What though her Father is a *Rogue,*
   Her Mother though a *Whore* is?
Thoſe *Vices* now are high in Vogue,
   And *Virtue* out of Door is.

III.

Great Dames there are, who break their Vows
   As oft as Madam *Peachum,*
And *greater Robbers* than her Spouſe,
   Though *Tyburn* cannot reach 'em.   6
What though *Macheath* too is as bad
   As Father or as Mother,
And, bleſt with *Polly,* is ſo mad
   To ramble to another?

IV.

Polly, I ween, is not the firſt,
   Nor will ſhe be the laſt, Sir,
Who in an Husband hath been curs'd,
   And met the ſame Diſaſter.
How many *Courtiers* have we known,
   Quite rotten ripe with Poxes,
Who, though they ſeldom wed but *One,*
   Keep half a Dozen *Doxies?*   7

V. But

---

4. *Faustina*: Faustina Bordoni and Francesca Cuzzoni (*Catsoni* in 1.10) were the
   two leading prima donnas; see introduction to 'Opera and Music'
5. *Senesino*: Francesco Bernardi Senesino, c.1680-c.1750, one of the most famous
   of 18th century castrati; he sang frequently in Handel's operas
6. *Tyburn*: the gallows
7. *Doxies*: mistresses

V.

But *Polly*'s not the worfe a Pin,
 Her Charms not lefs cœleftial;
But, though to *Rogues* and *Whores* a-kin,
 An Angel is terreftrial.
Some Prudes indeed, with envious Spight,
 Would blaft her Reputation,
And tell us that to *Ribands* bright
 She yields, upon Occafion.

VI.

But thefe are all invented Lies,
 And vile *outlandifh* Scandal,
Which from *Italian* Clubs arife,
 And Partizans of *Handel.*
Then let us toaft the blooming Lafs,
 Whofe Charms have thus enfnared me;
I'd drink it in a brimming Glafs,
8 Though Parfon * *H—rng* heard me.

---

 * A mighty weak fucking Prieft, who to fhow his Theological Capacity, preached a Sermon at *Lincoln's-Inn*-Chapel againft the *Deifm* of the Age, and the *Beggars Opera.*

---

8. *H_rng*: Herring, Dr. Thomas Herring; see introduction to 'The Morality Problem'

POLLY PEACHUM.

F all the Toasts, that *Britain* boasts;

    The Gim, the Gent, the Jolly,   1, 2

    The Brown, the Fair, the Debonair,

There's none cry'd up like POLLY;

She's fir'd the Town, has quite cut down

    The Opera of *Rolli*:   3

Go were you will, the Subject still,

    Is pretty, pretty POLLY.

There's Madam *Faustina*, Catso!   4, 5

    And eke Madame *Catsoni*;

Likewise *Signior Senesino*,   6

    Are *tutti Abbandonni* :   7

                      Ha,

"Polly Peachum," in Poems On Several Occasions. By H[enry] Carey. The Third Edition, much enlarged. London: Printed by E. Say, 1729. Pp. 151-153.

---

1. Gim: smart, spruce
2. Gent: graceful, elegant
3. *Rolli*: Paolo Antonio Rolli, librettist for the Italian opera in England
4. *Faustina*: Faustina Bordoni and Francesca Cuzzoni (*Catsoni* in 1.10) were the two leading primma donnas; see introduction to 'Opera and Music'
5. Catso: *cazzo* (Italian), vulgar for penis; simpleton
6. *Senesino*: Francesco Bernardi Senesino, c.1680-c. 1750, one of the most famous of 18th century castrati; he sang frequently in Handel's operas
7. *Abbandonni*: all abandoned

Ha, ha, ha, ha; *Do, re, mi, fa,*

 Are now but Farce and Folly,

We're ravish'd all, with Toll, loll, loll,

 And pretty! pretty POLLY.

8 The Sons of *Bayes,* in Lyric lays,

  Sound forth her Fame in Print O!

And, as we pass, in Frame and Glass,

9 We see her *Mezzo-tint*-O!

10 In *Ivy Lane,* the City strain,

  Is now no more on DOLLY;

11,12 And all the Brights, at *Man*'s and *White*'s

  Of nothing talk, but POLLY.

Ah! *Johnny Gay*! thy lucky Play,

 Has made the Criticks grin, a;

They cry 'tis flat, 'tis this, 'tis that,

 But let them Laugh that win, a:

X 2

---

8. *Bayes:* the foolish conceited dramatist in Buckingham's *The Rehearsal*; here the "Sons of Bayes" are poetasters

9. *Mezzo-tint*-O: a print made from a metal plate reproducing continuous tones of grey.

I swear *Parbleu*, 'tis naif and new,　　　　13

　　Ill Nature is but Folly;

'Thas lent a stitch to rent of RICH,　　　14

　　And set up Madam POLLY.

Ah Tuneful Fair! Beware! Beware!

　　Nor Toy with Star and Garter;

Fine Cloaths may hide a foul Inside,

　　And you may catch a Tartar:

If powder'd Fop, blow up your Shop,

'Twill make you Melancholy;

Then left to rot, you'll die forgot,

　　Alas! Alas! poor POLLY.

---

10. *Ivy-Lane*: street in the business section of London (to the east)
11. Brights: wits, dandies
12. *Man's* and *White's*: coffee houses in the fashionable section of London (to the west)
13. *Parbleu*: mild French oath
14. Rich: John Rich, manager of the Theatre Royal, Lincoln's Inn Fields, where *The Beggar's Opera* was first performed. The line puns on rent=tear in clothing and rent=income.

William Cooke, *Memoirs of Charles Macklin, Comedian* . . .
London, 1804, pp. 30-33.

The applause which he [Walker] obtained in Macheath, checked his progress as a general actor. His company, from this circumstance, was so eagerly sought after by the gay libertine young men of fashion, that he was scarcely ever sober, insomuch that we are told by the contemporary writers of that day, that he was frequently under the necessity of eating Sandwiches (or, as they were then called, anchovy toasts) behind the scenes, to alleviate the fumes of the liquor. . . . Davies, (Garrick's historian), who knew Walker personally, says, "He had from nature great advantages of voice and person: his countenance was manly and expressive; and the humour, ease, and gaiety, which he assumed in Macheath, and other characters of this complexion, rendered him a great favorite with the public. He knew little scientifically of music, other than singing a song in good ballad tune; but that singing was supported by a speaking eye, and inimitable action".

Suggested Readings

BATESON, F. W. *The English Comic Drama, 1700-1750*. Oxford: Clarendon Press, 1929.

BERGER, ARTHUR W. *"The Beggar's Opera*, the Burlesque, and Italian Opera." *Music and Letters*, XVII (1936), 93-105

BRONSON, BERTRAND. "The Beggar's Opera." Studies in the Comic (*University of California Publications in English*, Vol. VIII, No. 2), rpt. in John Loftis, ed. *Restoration Drama: Modern Essays in Criticism*. New York: Oxford University Press, 1966, pp. 298-327.

CLINTON-BADDELEY, V. C. *The Burlesque Tradition in the English Theatre after 1660*. London: Methuen, 1952.

EMPSON, WILLIAM. *Some Versions of Pastoral*, 1935; rpt. Norfolk, Connecticut: New Directions, 1960.

GAGEY, EDMOND. *Ballad Opera*. New York: Columbia University Press, 1937.

IRVING, WILLIAM HENRY. *John Gay. Favorite of the Wits*. Durham, North Carolina: Duke University Press, 1940.

IRWIN, WILLIAM. *The Making of Jonathan Wild*. New York: Columbia University Press, 1941.

KIDSON, F. W. *The Beggar's Opera. Its Predecessors and Successors*, 1922; rpt. Westport, Connecticut: Greenwood Press, 1971.

LOFTIS, JOHN. *The Politics of Drama in Augustan England*. Oxford: Clarendon Press, 1963.

NOBLE, YVONNE. *The Beggar's Opera: Twentieth Century Interpretations*. Englewood Cliffs, N.J.: Prentice-Hall, 1975.

SCHULTZ, William EBEN. *Gay's Beggar's Opera*, 1923; rpt. New York: Russell and Russell, 1967.

INDEX